best
easy
dayhikes

Mount St. Helens

Fred Barstad

FALCON®

HELENA, MONTANA

A FALCON GUIDE®

Falcon® Publishing is continually expanding its list of recreational guidebooks. All books include detailed descriptions, accurate maps, and all information necessary for enjoyable trips. You can order extra copies of this book and get information and prices for other Falcon® books by writing Falcon, P.O. Box 1718, Helena, MT 59624 or calling toll free 1-800-582-2665. Also, please ask for a free copy of our current catalog. Visit our website at www.FalconOutdoors.com or contact us via e-mail at www.falconguide.com.

© 1999 Falcon® Publishing, Inc., Helena, Montana.
Printed in Canada.

1 2 3 4 5 6 7 8 9 0 TP 05 04 03 02 01 00 99

Falcon and FalconGuide are registered trademarks of Falcon® Publishing, Inc.

All rights reserved, including the right to reproduce this book or parts thereof, in any form, except for the inclusion of brief quotations in a review.

Cataloging-in-Publication Data is on record at the Library of Congress.

CAUTION

Outdoor recreational activities are by their very nature potentially hazardous. All participants in such activities must assume responsibility for their own actions and safety. The information contained in this guidebook cannot replace sound judgment and good decision-making skills, which help reduce risk exposure, nor does the scope of this book allow for disclosure of all the potential hazards and risks involved in such activities.

Learn as much as possible about the outdoor recreational activities in which you participate, prepare for the unexpected, and be cautious. The reward will be a safer and more enjoyable experience.

 Text pages printed on recycled paper.

Contents

Map Legend v

Overview Map vi

Introduction 1

Ranking the Hikes 3

Leave No Trace 4

Western Region: Access from Washington 504

  1 Hummocks Loop 7

  2 Birth of a Lake Loop 11

  3 Coldwater Lake 13

  4 South Coldwater 17

  5 Boundary Trail (Johnston Ridge–
     Hummocks Trailhead) 21

  6 Eruption Loop 24

  7 Harry's Ridge 27

Southern Region: Access from Cougar, Washington

  8 Sheep Canyon–Crescent Ridge Loop 33

  9 Goat Marsh 37

 10 Lower Ape Cave 39

 11 Trail of Two Forests 43

 12 Ptarmigan Trail 47

 13 June Lake 51

 14 Ape Canyon 53

 15 Lava Canyon 57

Eastern Region: Access from Forest Road 99

16 Ghost Lake 63
17 Plains of Abraham Loop 67
18 Independence Loop 73
19 Harmony Trail 79
20 Independence Pass (South Segment) 83
21 Meta Lake 87
22 Ryan Lake Loop 89

Along Forest Road 25

23 Cedar Flats Nature Trail Loop 93
24 Iron Creek Falls 97
25 Woods Creek Watchable Wildlife Loop 99

Map Legend

Interstate	(26)	Campground	▲	
US Highway	(17)	Bridge		
State or Other Principal Road	(66) (690)	Cabins/Buildings	▪	
Forest Service Road	708	Elevation	3,294 ft. x	
Interstate Highway	⟹	Gate	•—•	
Paved Road	⟹	Mine Site	⚒	
Gravel Road	⟹	Overlook/Point of Interest	▫	
Unimproved Road	======⟹	Restricted Area		
Trailhead/Parking	◯ Ⓟ	National Volcanic Monument Boundary		
Starting Point	◯			
One Way Road	One Way →	Map Orientation	N	
Described trail				
Secondary Trail		Scale	0 0.5 1	
River/Creek/Falls			Miles	
Lake/Pond				
Boardwalk	‖‖‖‖‖‖‖‖‖			

Overview

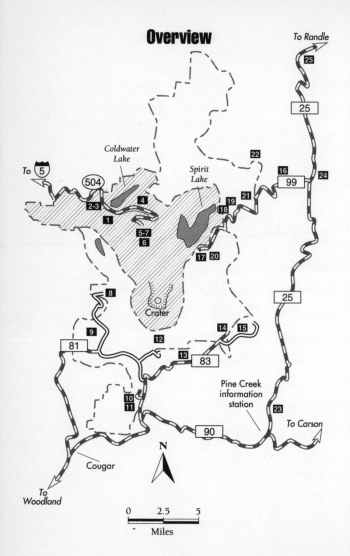

Introduction

Best Easy Day Hikes Mount St. Helens is a much-shortened version of *Hiking Mount St. Helens*. Many people have asked me for a smaller guidebook that is better suited to the more casual hiker. *Best Easy Day Hikes Mount St. Helens* is just that book. As I hiked the trails and wrote *Hiking Mount St. Helens,* I noted the easily accessible and less strenuous hikes that would appeal to most visitors.

Hiking Mount St. Helens covers nearly all the trails in and leading into Mount St. Helens National Volcanic Monument. This includes trails that are not the most scenic and definitely not easy.

Most of the hikes in Best Easy Day Hikes Mount St. Helens are short—less than 8 miles round trip—and, with a few exceptions, have less than 1000 feet of elevation gain or loss. Many are short and easy enough for families with small children, and a couple are barrier-free, making them wheelchair accessible. All the trailheads are easily accessible with a passenger car; all but three have paved roads leading to them.

The hikes in this book are rated on their difficulty. When you are trying to decide which hike to take, check the ranking chart first to see if the hike will be suitable for all the members of your party.

Types of Hikes

Loop: A loop hike starts and ends at the same trailhead. There may be a part of the hike that retraces the same route

1

for a short distance. The mileage given for a loop hike is the total distance from the starting point back to the same point.

Out and back: Out and back hikes go to a specific destination and return via the same route. The mileage given for an out and back hike is the sum of both the outbound and the return trips.

Shuttle: A shuttle hike requires a car shuttle between trailheads. The mileage given is the distance between the starting point and the ending point of the hike.

Maps

The map referred to as MSHNVM in most of the hike descriptions is the USDA Forest Service Mount St. Helens National Volcanic Monument map. This topographic map (aka The Brown Map) has a picture of a waterfall on the cover.

Ranking the Hikes

Easiest
  11   Trail of Two Forests (barrier-free)
   2   Birth of a Lake Loop (barrier-free)
  21   Meta Lake
  24   Iron Creek Falls
   6   Eruption Loop (barrier-free)
  23   Cedar Flats Nature Trail
  22   Ryan Lake Loop
   9   Goat Marsh
  25   Woods Creek Watchable Wildlife Loop
   1   Hummocks Loop
  13   June Lake
   3   Coldwater Lake
  10   Ape Cave (underground hike)
  20   Independence Pass Trail (South Segment)
  16   Ghost Lake
  19   Harmony Trail
   7   Harry's Ridge
  18   Independence Loop
  12   Ptarmigan Trail
   5   Boundary Trail (Johnston Ridge–Hummocks Trailhead)
   4   South Coldwater
  14   Ape Canyon
  17   Plains of Abraham Loop
   8   Sheep Canyon–Crescent Ridge Loop
  15   Lava Canyon (Difficult after the first 0.3
Hardest   mile, first 0.2 mile is barrier-free.)

Leave No Trace

Mount St. Helens National Volcanic Monument is a landscape in a constant state of change and rejuvenation. It is a natural laboratory for studying the recuperative powers of nature after a volcanic eruption. For this reason, closely following the regulations is of the utmost importance. Don't leave the trail while you are in the restricted zone. Leave all natural features as you found them; this includes not taking a chunk of pumice home with you. Look at the flowers but don't pick or trample them. Dispose of human waste properly. Pack out all your trash and any other trash you find.

Cutting switchbacks is extremely hard on trails and hillsides. This practice causes much erosion and destroys plant life. It is always best to stay on the trail and not take shortcuts. It also usually takes less energy to follow the trail. Where the trail is braided try to stay on the main route. Do not dismantle rock cairns as they may be the only things marking the route in some areas.

A great source of information about the techniques of leaving no trace is the FalconGuide *Leave No Trace* by Will Harmon (Falcon, 1997). This book can be found at many bookstores or may be ordered directly from Falcon Publishing.

We all need to do our part to keep our wild areas beautiful and clean forever.

Western Region
Access from Washington 504

The old twisting asphalt ribbon of Washington 504, up the Toutle River Valley from Interstate 5, was used for decades as the main access route to Spirit Lake and the slopes of Mount St. Helens. The route endures today though its location and character are much changed.

As you approach the mountain the new highway leaves the valley floor. By the time you get to Coldwater Ridge Visitors Center, 43 miles from I-5 you are well within the Blast Zone, and high above the debris filled Toutle River Valley. Past Coldwater Ridge the route descends to the foot of Coldwater Lake, a lake that was formed when the Debris Avalanche dammed the mouth of Coldwater Creek Canyon. From trailheads near the foot of the lake Hummocks Trail (Hike 1) explores the debris filled Toutle River Valley and Birth of a Lake Trail (Hike 2) takes you along the shore and out over the waters of Coldwater lake.

The highway then follows the South Fork of Coldwater Creek up to its headwaters, passing South Coldwater Trailhead, before climbing the last couple of miles to the top of Johnston Ridge and the Johnston Ridge Observatory. The observatory parking area is the trailhead for Boundary Trail (Hike 5). The popular and sometimes crowded plaza next to the observatory is the trail head for Eruption Loop (Hike 6) and Harry's Ridge (Hike 7).

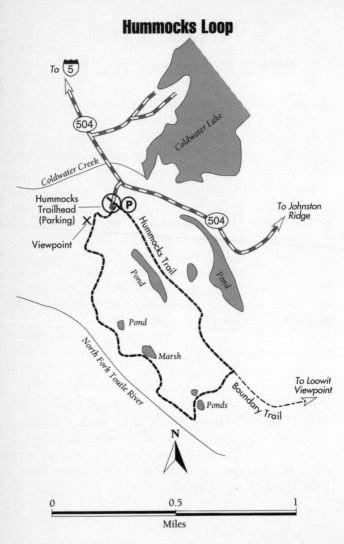

Hummocks Loop

To [5]

504

Coldwater Creek

Coldwater Lake

Hummocks
Trailhead
(Parking)

P

Viewpoint

Hummocks Trail

504

To Johnston
Ridge

Pond

Pond

Pond

North Fork Toutle River

Pond

Marsh

Ponds

Boundary Trail

To Loowit
Viewpoint

N

0   0.5   1

Miles

1
HUMMOCKS LOOP

Type of hike: Loop.
Total distance: 2.3 miles.
Elevation gain: Minimal.
Maps: MSHNVM. Elk Rock USGS quad covers the area but does not show this trail.
Starting Point: Hummocks Trailhead.

Finding the trailhead: Hummocks Trailhead is located 2.4 miles southeast of Coldwater Ridge Visitors Center on Washington 504. To reach it from Portland or Seattle, take Exit 49 from Interstate 5 (49 miles north of the Columbia River Bridge or 120 miles south of Seattle.). Drive 45 miles east on WA 504, to the trailhead on the right side of the highway. There is a sign marking the trailhead. There are really two trailheads for this loop trail. They are about 50 yards apart at this parking area. GPS coordinates are 46 17.176N 122 16.306W.

Key points:
0.2 Viewpoint of Coldwater Creek Canyon.
0.7 Marsh.
1.6 Junction with Boundary Trail.

The hike: To hike the loop in a counter-clockwise direction, as described here, leave the Hummocks Trail parking area at its west end. At first the trail climbs a few feet over the mudflow debris. The path then bears right heading north-west and soon begins to descend. A couple of hundred yards from the parking area you make a switchback to the left in a grove of thick young alders. Note the damage caused by elk rubbing their antlers against and chewing on the young trees.

A short distance farther along there is a view to the right of the new canyon dug by Coldwater Creek. There is a short path to the right here but regulations require that hikers stay on the main trail. The tread passes a pond 0.3 mile past the viewpoint, and soon comes alongside of a cattail-filled marsh. After passing the marsh you cross a stream and the North Fork Toutle River comes into view, 150 yards to the right. The trail is now heading southeast with Mount St. Helens in view ahead.

The trail follows the riverbed bank (well away from the river) for 0.2 mile. It then bears left (northeast) and climbs passing a couple of ponds. Watch for ducks in the ponds and for elk nearby. A small wooden bridge that may be flooded in spring eases the stream crossing between the ponds. The trail climbs gently after passing the ponds. It passes another pond and comes to the junction with Boundary Trail 0.3 mile from the bridge.

At the junction, Boundary Trail (Hike 5) leads off to the right (southeast). Hummocks Trail turns to the left and heads northwest. Follow this route from the junction back 0.7 mile to the parking area. On the way, the tread passes a couple more ponds before re-entering the parking area at its southeast corner.

Elk are very common along this trail in the spring, I saw more than 100 of them when I hiked this trail in April.

Options: Hike Birth of a Lake Trail (Hike 2) after you have completed this hike. The trailheads are close together.

Birth of a Lake Trail

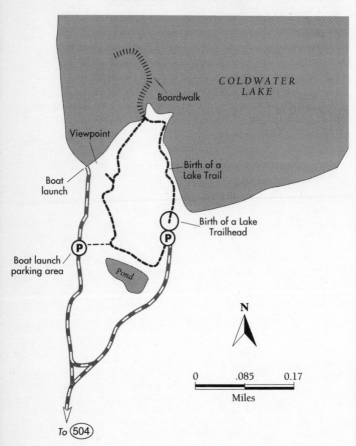

COLDWATER LAKE

Boardwalk

Viewpoint

Birth of a Lake Trail

Boat launch

Birth of a Lake Trailhead

Boat launch parking area

Pond

N

0   .085   0.17
Miles

To (504)

2
BIRTH OF A LAKE LOOP

Type of hike: Loop.
Total distance: 0.5 mile.
Elevation gain: Minimal.
Maps: None required; look at the map at the trailhead and the one in this book.
Starting point: Birth of a Lake Trailhead.

Finding the trailhead: The Birth of a Lake Trailhead is located 2.2 miles southeast of the Coldwater Ridge Visitors Center on Washington 504. To reach it from Portland or Seattle take Exit 49 from Interstate 5 (49 miles north of the Columbia River Bridge or 120 miles south of Seattle). Drive 45 miles east on WA 504, to the sign pointing left to the Coldwater Recreation Area. Turn left, then bear right at the Y intersection to reach the trailhead which is 0.1 mile from the highway. GPS coordinates at the trailhead are 4617.204N 122 15.895W.

Key points:
0.1   Junction with boardwalk.
0.3   Path to boat launch.

The hike: The Birth of a Lake Loop is a barrier-free interpretive loop path along the shore of and over Coldwater Lake. The paved trail leaves the parking area at its north end next to a signboard with a map of the area. As you work your way along the lakeshore for 250 yards you will see several interpretive signs. These signs explain the formation of the lake after the 1980 eruption of Mount St. Helens. Take the time to turn right (north) at the junction, and walk out over the shallow waters of the lake to points of interest out there.

Back on the main trail, continue on past a viewpoint and the path to the boat launch area to the south end of the parking area where you started. You climb over a small rise between the path to the boat launch and the parking area.

Options: Hike this short loop after you have finished hiking Hike 1; the trailheads are close together.

3
COLDWATER LAKE
(AKA LAKES TRAIL)

Type of hike: Out and back.
Total distance: 7.6 miles.
Elevation gain: Minimal.
Maps: MSHNVM. Elk Rock and Spirit Lake West USGS quads cover the area but don't show this trail.
Starting point: Coldwater Lake Recreation Area Boat Launch and Trailhead (aka Lakes Trailhead)

Finding the trail: The trail starts at the boat launch at the foot of Coldwater Lake, located 2.2 miles southeast of the Coldwater Ridge Visitors Center on Washington 504. To reach it from Portland or Seattle take Exit 49 from Interstate 5 (49 miles north of the Columbia River Bridge or 120 miles south of Seattle). Drive 45 miles east on WA 504, to the sign pointing left to the Coldwater Recreation Area. Turn left, and then bear left at the Y intersection to reach the trailhead, which is 0.1 mile from the highway. GPS coordinates at the trailhead are 46 17.481N 122 16.018W.

Key points:
0.7   Junction with Elk Bench Trail.
1.0   Lake access.
3.8   Lake access at head of Coldwater Lake.

Coldwater Lake, South Coldwater

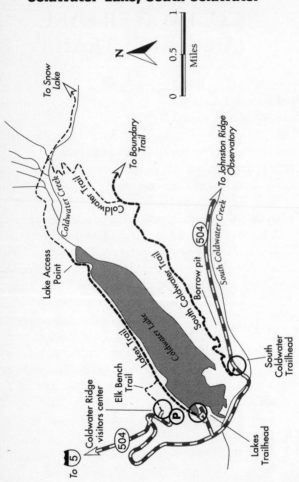

The hike: Leave the boat launch and follow the paved trail for a short distance, then bear left on the marked path. You will wind in and out of a couple of side draws with small seasonal streams as you make your way along the lakeshore. Reach the junction with the Elk Bench Trail 0.7 mile from the trailhead and well above the lakeshore. The Elk Bench Trail turns off to the left and climbs to the west to the Coldwater Ridge Visitors Center.

From the junction continue along the lakeshore for another 0.3 mile to a spot where lake access is allowed. The lake access is marked with signs and there is a restroom to the left of the trail. This is one of only two points along the shore of the lake where hikers can leave the trail—and then for only a short distance between the marked boundaries. Cottonwoods are beginning to reforest this area; there are some relatively large ones here close to the trail.

After passing the lake access point, the trail crosses more streams and traverses a grove of young alder. As you pass the alder and cottonwood trees look for the evidence of chewing beavers. At 0.8 mile past the lake access point you will cross a stream with a waterfall that drops in stages from the ridge above the trail. Just past this waterfall the trail climbs slightly and passes below some dark cliffs. The route soon descends back to near lake level, then climbs again to traverse above another set of cliffs. As you pass these cliffs another waterfall descends the slope to your left.

A bit farther along a view of the canyon ahead opens up as you pass through alder thickets and cross tiny streams. The rubbing and chewing activities of elk have scarred many of the young alder trees along this part of the trail.

Watch for them on all the open slopes around the lake. The trail reaches the lake access point at the head of Coldwater Lake 3.8 miles from the trailhead. There is no restroom available here.

This hike is best done early in the season. Many of the streams may be dry by midsummer. When I hiked this trail in mid-April I had elk in view much of the time.

Options: Use the Elk Bench Trail to gain access to this hike from the Coldwater Ridge Visitors Center, and make a short car shuttle to the Lakes Trailhead.

4
SOUTH COLDWATER

see map page 14

Type of hike: Out and back.
Total distance: 6.8 miles.
Elevation gain: 1,380 feet.
Maps: MSHNVM. Elk Rock and Spirit Lake West USGS quads cover the area but do not show these trails.
Starting point: South Coldwater Trailhead.

Finding the trailhead: To reach the South Coldwater Trailhead from Portland or Seattle take Exit 49 from Interstate 5 (49 miles north of the Columbia River Bridge or 120 miles south of Seattle). Drive 46 miles east on Washington 504, to the trailhead. The signed trailhead is on the left of the highway, 3.3 miles southeast of the Coldwater Ridge Visitors Center. GPS coordinates at the trailhead are 46 17.144N 122 15 .239W.

Key points:
3.4   Junction with Coldwater Trail.

The hike: The South Coldwater Trail leaves from the southwest corner of the parking area. The path climbs gently on a slope through scattered willows. Stumps between the willows and the general lack of downed trees show that this area was logged before the 1980 eruption. Shortly, as you round a poorly defined ridge, the Coldwater Ridge Visitors

Center and Coldwater Lake come into view to the north-west. If you hike this section of trail in late spring you will probably see elk. This is winter range for the large animals; by June most of them have left for the higher country to the northeast. Follow the route, that is marked with posts, and cross an abandoned roadbed 0.5 mile from the trailhead. This roadbed, like all of the abandoned roads on this hill is badly drifted in with pumice. The path makes a switchback to the right then crosses the rounded ridgeline. On the ridgeline you make a wide switchback to the left as you cross another roadbed.

As you climb along the ridge you will pass much evidence of pre-eruption logging in the form of roads and skid trails. An abandoned borrow pit is passed 1.3 miles from the trailhead. This pit, at 3,150 feet elevation, was dug to furnish rock for the construction of the logging roads. It is marked on the quad map. The tread passes the remains of a portable spar pole 0.8 mile after passing the borrow pit. This broken and twisted equipment shows the tremendous force of the 1980 eruption. A logging operation was in progress in this area at the time of the eruption. It is easy to pick out the sections that were not yet logged at the time of the blast by the thousands of logs that now lie on the ground. A short distance past the portable spar pole is a half-buried caterpillar tractor.

For the next mile the route generally follows another abandoned roadbed. The tread traverses along the left side of the ridgeline to the junction with Coldwater Trail. This junction, at 3,830 feet elevation, is 3.4 miles from South Coldwater Trailhead.

Options: For a longer loop hike, turn left on the Coldwater Trail and follow it to the Lakes Trail. Then turn left again and head southwest on the Lakes Trail. The Lakes Trail follows the shoreline of Coldwater Lake to the Lakes Trailhead in the Coldwater Recreation Area. From the Lakes Trailhead it is a little over a mile along the Coldwater Recreation Area access road and WA 504 back to the South Coldwater Trailhead. Hike 3 covers the section of the Lakes Trail along Coldwater Lake.

Boundary Trail

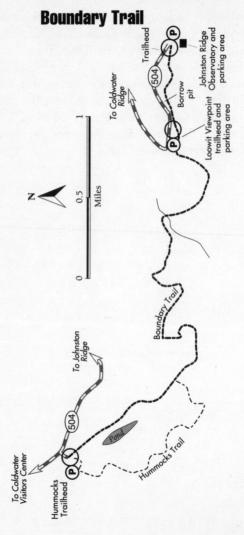

5
BOUNDARY TRAIL
(JOHNSTON RIDGE TO
HUMMOCKS TRAILHEAD)

Type of hike: Shuttle.
Total distance: 4.3 miles.
Elevation loss: 1,680 feet.
Maps: MSHNVM. Spirit Lake East and Elk Rock USGS quads covers the area but do not show this trail.
Starting point: Johnston Ridge Observatory parking area.

Finding the trailhead: From Portland, head north on Interstate 5, from Seattle head south on I-5. Take Exit 49 from I-5 (49 miles north of the Columbia River Bridge or 120 miles south of Seattle) then follow Washington 504 for 52 miles east to the Johnston Ridge Observatory parking area. The observatory is at the end of WA 504. The trail leaves from the west corner of the large parking area. The GPS coordinates are 46 16.500N 122 13.050W.

Key points:
0.6   Loowit Viewpoint. GPS 46 16.663N 122 13.765W.
3.6   Junction with Hummocks Trail.
4.3   Hummocks Trailhead. GPS 46 17.176N 122 16.306W.

The hike: The trail crosses the highway and then climbs a few feet to the ridgeline of Johnston Ridge. Lupine and fireweed grow from the pumice-covered landscape. The path soon descends along the south side of the ridge in full view of Mount St. Helens, the Pumice Desert and the grassy benchlands along the North Fork Toutle River Valley. Small huckleberry and elderberry bushes grow up between the stumps. Penstemon blooms here in July and in August pearly everlasting blooms appear. Half a mile from the parking area you will reach an old borrow pit. Just past the pit is the Loowit Trailhead and Viewpoint parking area. The route, which is paved for a short distance, skirts the parking area along its south side.

After leaving the paved parking area at the Loowit View-point, the Boundary Trail traverses the volcanically blasted slope to the west. You cross a spur ridge 0.3 mile from the Loowit Viewpoint Trailhead. Blacktail deer as well as elk frequent this spur ridge. You will probably see their tracks on the trail and may get a glimpse of them moving away at your approach. Castle Lake is in view ahead to the south-west. Castle Lake was formed by the eruption of Mount St. Helens in 1980 and the resulting mudflow that dammed the South Fork Castle Creek.

After crossing the spur the trail heads northwest. Soon Coldwater Lake, another lake that was formed by the erup-tion, comes into view ahead. The Coldwater Visitors Center can be seen on the far side of the lake on Coldwater Ridge. The path heads northwest for 0.2 mile, crossing a tiny stream that may be dry by summer, then bears to the left (west). The tread soon crosses a flat area; posts mark the trail here as it may be hard to spot on the ground. Past the flat area the trail continues gently down a stump-and-bracken fern–covered slope for 0.3 mile. The route then makes a switchback to the left, then one to the right at the edge of a steep canyon as it descends. It then follows a long-abandoned roadbed for a short distance. Bearing left off the roadbed the path crosses a gentle slope to another abandoned road. The route follows this road-bed south for 0.1 mile then makes a switchback to the left and descends east to the base of the ridge.

Once off the steep sided hill the trail crosses the mud-flow debris southeast and south before turning west toward the junction with the Hummocks Trail. From here to the junction the trail is marked with posts. The route descends a gully, then crosses a grassy meadow with a pond to your left and soon meets the Hummocks Trail. Beyond the junction at 2,520 feet elevation, the Hummocks Trail and the Boundary Trail share the same route. Bear right (really straight ahead to the northwest) on the Hummocks Trail and follow it 0.7 miles to the Hummocks Trailhead and parking area.

Options: The return trip can be made back up the same route to Johnston Ridge Observatory, but it is better to make a car shuttle between the trailheads. Hiking the Hummocks Loop is a nice addition to this hike. See Hike 1 for directions to the Hummocks Trailhead and a description of the Hummocks Loop hike.

6
ERUPTION LOOP

Type of hike: Loop.
Total distance: 0.5 mile.
Elevation gain: Minimal.
Maps: No map is needed for this short, paved loop. There is a map on a signboard at the beginning of the trail.
Starting point: Johnston Ridge Observatory Plaza.

Finding the trailhead: From Portland, head north on Interstate 5; from Seattle, head south on I-5. Take Exit 49 from I-5 (49 miles north of the Columbia River Bridge or 120 miles south of Seattle) then follow Washington 504 for 52 miles, to Johnston Ridge Observatory at the end of the highway. Walk up the wide paved trail from the parking area to the observatory. Eruption Trail will be to your left as you reach the observatory.

Key points:
0.2   Cul-de-sac at top of hill.
0.3   Junction with Boundary Trail.
0.4   Parking area.

The hike: The Eruption Loop starts at the east edge of the paved outdoor plaza next to the Johnston Ridge Observatory. The trail climbs gently, making three switchbacks, then winds up to an interpretive sign about stumps. Half-

Eruption Loop

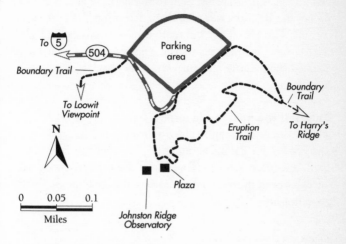

buried logs, penstemon and fireweed line the route. Shortly you will come to another interpretive sign, this one about the Debris Avalanche. There is a paved cul-de-sac to the left of the trail 0.2 mile from the trailhead where a third sign discusses new magma. At 4,310 feet elevation, this is the highest point on this trail.

The trail descends from the cul-de-sac, passing another interpretive sign about change. Pearly everlasting flowers crowd this part of the trail in August. After the trail makes a switchback to the right, Coldwater Peak looms ahead. The Spillover, where the Debris Avalanche crossed over the top of Johnston Ridge, can be seen to the east. Beyond The Spillover is Harry's Ridge. The trail makes a switchback to the left at the junction with the Boundary Trail, 0.3 mile from the trailhead. From here to the parking area 0.1 mile ahead, the Boundary Trail and the Eruption Trail are concurrent. The exit of the tunnel that now drains Spirit Lake can be seen below next to the highway. Once you have reached the parking area turn left to get back to the observatory.

Options: If you want to add some distance to your hike, walk out the Boundary Trail to The Spillover or to Harry's Ridge. See Hike 7 for details about this section of the Boundary Trail and Harry's Ridge Trail. Take the time to check out the exhibits in the observatory and see the great movie about the eruption.

7
HARRY'S RIDGE

Type of hike: Out and back.
Total distance: 8.4 miles.
Elevation gain: 600 feet.
Maps: MSHNVM. Spirit Lake West and Elk Rock USGS quads cover the area but don't show the trail.
Starting point: Johnston Ridge Observatory parking area.

Finding the trailhead: To reach Johnston Ridge Observatory from Portland or Seattle take Exit 49 from Interstate 5 (49 miles north of the Columbia River Bridge or 120 miles south of Seattle). Drive east on Washington 504 for 52 miles to the highway's end at the observatory. GPS coordinates are 46 16.505N 122 13.040W.

Key points:
2.5 Junction with Truman Trail. GPS 46 16.458N 122 11.014W.
3.6 Junction with Harry's Ridge Trail. GPS 46 16.900N 122 10.370W.
4.2 Viewpoints on Harry's Ridge.

The hike: The hike to Harry's Ridge begins on the Boundary Trail. The Boundary Trail heads east from the east corner of the parking area. For the first 250 yards, the Boundary Trail and the Eruption Trail follow the same paved route. The path

Harry's Ridge

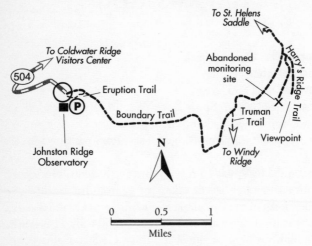

then bears left off the Eruption Trail at a switchback to continue southeast. Here Mount St. Helens and the Pumice Plain come into full view to the south.

The Boundary Trail descends gently along the flower-covered ridge for a short distance. After losing about 150 feet in elevation the path flattens out, and even climbs in a few spots. You will generally follow the ridgeline for the next 0.8 mile. Then the route makes a right turn to head south across a steep hillside. Keep your head and hang on to your children here. This traverse crosses a very steep and loose slope. A slip off the right side of the route could result in disaster. The traverse lasts for 0.3 mile then the tread turns left to cross a spur ridge.

As it crosses the spur ridge, the route turns to the northeast. You now traverse a gentler slope for 0.5 mile to the junction with the Truman Trail. Mount Adams and Spirit Lake are in view to the right along this traverse. The junction with the Truman Trail, at 4,150 feet elevation, is 2.5 miles from the Johnston Ridge Observatory. The Truman Trail crosses the Pumice Plain to the Windy Ridge Viewpoint, 5.9 miles away.

As you leave the junction with the Truman Trail the path climbs to the northeast, reaching the ridgeline at Spillover Saddle. The Spillover is where the Debris Avalanche, which immediately preceded the May 1980 eruption, crossed over the top of Johnston Ridge and descended into South Coldwater Canyon. The hummocks on both sides of the trail were once part of the pre-1980 Mount St. Helens. The route crosses Spillover Saddle then traverses around the head of a basin to the junction with the Harry's Ridge Trail.

The junction with Harry's Ridge Trail, at 4,380 feet elevation, is 3.6 miles from the Johnston Ridge Observatory. Harry's Ridge is named for Harry Truman, the lodge owner at the south end of Spirit Lake who died in the 1980 eruption.

At the signed junction turn right on Harry's Ridge Trail and climb to the east. For the first 0.2 mile, the cairn-marked trail winds up a hillside covered with flowers and blasted-off stumps. Then you have a choice to make: you can follow the post-lined path across the ridgeline then traverse the east-facing slope for 0.4 mile to a viewpoint, or you can bear slightly right (south) on the unmaintained path to follow the ridgeline to its highest point, 0.4 mile away.

In either case Mount Adams is in view to the east, and from either viewpoint the panoramic view is spectacular in all directions. To the south is the crater of Mount St. Helens, with the nearly black Lava Dome bulging in its center. Spirit Lake and Windy Ridge are to the east. The rugged peaks of the Mount Margaret Backcountry are to the north, and to the west is the devastated area along the Toutle River. There is an abandoned volcano-monitoring site on the top of Harry's Ridge.

Options: On the return trip it adds only 0.3 mile to turn left on Eruption Loop and follow it to Johnston Ridge Observatory before returning to the parking area.

Southern Region
Access from Cougar, Washington

This lush side of Mount St. Helens National Volcanic Monument was little affected by the 1980 eruption. Old and second-growth forests cover most of the area.

The southern region however has no lack of volcanic features. Over the centuries lava flows have streamed from the mountain in many places. In some of these flows lava tube caves were formed. Hike 10 explores the largest of these caves.

Lahars did rush down several of the canyons on the south side of the mountain during the 1980 eruption, wiping out nearly everything in their path. Hike 14 takes you to the largest of these lahars. Hike 15, Lava Canyon, descends through a canyon that was scoured by one of the lahars to expose some of the prettiest waterfalls to be found anywhere.

The Southern Region of Mount St. Helens National Volcanic Monument is used in all seasons. Marked cross-country ski trails and snowmobile trails crisscross this region. Cougar and Marble Mountain Snoparks are maintained throughout the winter to provide easy access.

Sheep Canyon-Crescent Ridge Loop

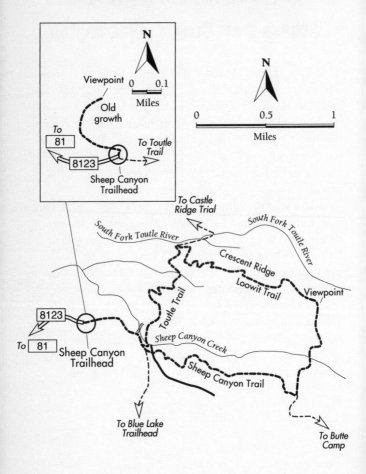

8
SHEEP CANYON–
CRESCENT RIDGE LOOP

Type of hike: Loop.
Total distance: 7 miles.
Elevation gain: 1,260 feet.
Maps: MSHNVM. Goat Mountain and Mount St. Helens USGS quads cover the area but do not show these trails.
Starting point: Sheep Canyon Trailhead.

Finding the trailhead: From Portland or Seattle take Interstate 5 to Exit 21 (21 miles north of the Columbia River Bridge or 150 miles south of Seattle) at Woodland. Drive east for 26.5 miles on Washington 503 (which becomes WA 503 spur) to the junction with Forest Road 81. Turn left (north) and follow FR 81 for 11.3 miles to the junction with FR 8123. Turn left on Forest Road 8123 and drive north 6.5 miles to the Sheep Canyon Trailhead at the end of the road. FR 8123 is a gravel road.

Key points:
0.6   First junction with Toutle Trail. GPS 46 12.001N 122 15.586W.
2.3   Junction with Loowit Trail.
4.9   Junction with Toutle Trail in South Fork Toutle River Canyon. GPS 46 12.607N 122 15.179W.
6.4   Junction with Sheep Canyon Trail.

The hike: As you leave the trailhead the route climbs gently through a brushy area. Beside the path lupine and other flowers add color. Soon the tread enters old-growth forest. The trail skirts the edge of Sheep Canyon 0.5 mile from the trailhead. Here a side path goes to the left a short distance to a viewpoint of a waterfall in Sheep Canyon Creek.

Just past the viewpoint is the first junction with the Toutle Trail. Bear right at the junction and continue to climb. For a short distance here the Toutle Trail and the Sheep Canyon Trail follow the same route. The Toutle Trail splits off to the right 0.7 mile from the trailhead. Bear left (almost straight ahead) at this junction and cross a single-log bridge. A few yards after crossing the bridge there is a good campsite on the right side of the trail.

For the next 0.9 mile the trail winds its way up the ridge on the south side of Sheep Canyon. When you are away from the edge of the canyon you climb through old growth forest, but close to the rim the forest was stripped away by the mudflow from the 1980 eruption. The route bears to the right away from the canyon 1.7 miles from the trailhead. Now, at about 4,200 feet elevation, the composition of the forest begins to change. The trees are smaller and spaced farther apart. Huckleberries grow thickly between the trees. If you are here in late August you may want to take the time to enjoy their fruit.

The trail crosses a gully two-tenths of a mile after leaving the rim of Sheep Canyon. It then climbs out onto an old lava flow. From here the route winds its way up through thinning timber to the junction with the Loowit Trail at 4,600 feet elevation, 2.3 miles from the Sheep Canyon Trailhead. At this junction turning right will take you to Butte Camp.

Turn left on the Loowit Trail and head north. In a short distance the trail descends a little and crosses Sheep Canyon. Sheep Canyon Creek flows down the center of the canyon. The canyon is much broader here than it was down below. The route climbs a flower-covered slope leaving the canyon. Shortly after leaving the canyon the trail enters The Blast Zone. One mile from the junction with the Sheep Canyon Trail a great viewpoint on the right side of the trail overlooks the South Fork Toutle River Canyon.

At the viewpoint the trail turns to the northwest and begins the long descent of Crescent Ridge. The route winds and switchbacks its way down, losing 1,400 feet in elevation in the next 1.6 miles. The descent route down Crescent Ridge is along the edge of The Blast Zone. At times you walk through blown-down timber and at others you are in old growth forest.

The route reaches another junction with the Toutle Trail 4.9 miles from the trailhead at the bottom of Crescent Ridge. At this junction near the South Fork Toutle River the Loowit Trail turns to the right. Turn left and follow the Toutle Trail climbing to the southwest. The trail climbs for 1.5 miles to the junction with the Sheep Canyon Trail, completing the loop. At the junction with the Sheep Canyon Trail turn right (northwest) and retrace your steps for 0.6 mile to the Sheep Canyon Trailhead.

Options: A much shorter option is to hike from the trailhead to Sheep Canyon Viewpoint. The viewpoint trail leaves from the north side of the parking area directly across from the Sheep Canyon Trail. The viewpoint is reached in 0.3 mile, after passing through a short section of open, old-growth forest. See map insert.

Goat Marsh

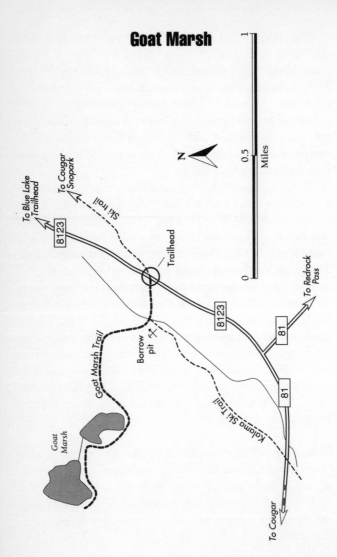

9
GOAT MARSH

Type of hike: Out and back.
Total distance: 2.8 miles.
Elevation gain: Minimal.
Maps: USGS Goat Mountain quad.
Starting Point: The junction of Kalama Ski Trail and FR 8123.

Finding the trailhead: From Exit 21 (approximately 150 miles south of Seattle or 21 miles north of the Columbia River Bridge) on Interstate 5 at Woodland, drive east on Washington 503 (which becomes WA 503 spur). Turn left (north) off WA 503 spur 26.5 miles from I-5 on Forest Road 81. Follow FR 81 for 11.3 miles to the junction with FR 8123. Turn left on FR 8123 and drive north 0.6 mile to the point where the Kalama Ski Trail crosses the road. There is a sign at the junction. FR 8123 is a gravel road.

Key points:
0.2 Leave Kalama Ski Trail and join Goat Marsh Trail. GPS 46 09.251N 122 16.251W.
0.9 First lake.
1.4 End of trail next to second lake.

The hike: Much of Goat Marsh Trail is really an abandoned roadbed that is nicely reverting to a trail. Hike west on the Kalama Ski Trail for 0.2 mile to the junction with

Goat Marsh Trail. Turn right at the junction and head north-west through hemlock forest. The route passes an abandoned borrow pit and soon comes to a wooden fence with a gate. The fence and gate are here to prevent motor vehicles from continuing to Goat Marsh. The route climbs very gently at first, then levels out. For the first 0.9 mile, the route is marked with blue diamond cross-country ski trail markers.

As you near the first lake the hiking trail bears left off the marked ski trail. The roadbed soon ends and the poorly marked trail traverses around the south side of the lake. As the trail leaves the first lake it passes a beaver dam. The path soon reaches the south side of another shallow lake. It works its way around to the southeast corner of this second lake and ends in the forest near the shore.

Options: Many elk inhabit Goat Marsh. Hike this trail early in the morning and watch for them in the open areas north of the lakes.

10
LOWER APE CAVE

Type of hike: Out and back.
Total distance: 1.7 miles.
Elevation loss: Minimal.
Maps: MSHNVM and Mount Mitchell USGS quad show the main entrance to the cave.
Starting point: Ape Cave parking area.

Finding the trailhead: Head north from Portland on Interstate 5 to Exit 21 at Woodland, Washington. From Seattle, drive south on I-5 to Exit 21, approximately 150 miles. Then follow Washington 503 (which becomes WA 503 spur) for 27.5 miles east to Cougar. From Cougar drive east on WA 503 spur (which becomes Forest Road 90) for 6.8 miles then turn left (north) on FR 83. Follow FR 83 for 2 miles then turn left again on FR 8303. Follow FR 8303 for 1 mile north to the parking area and trailhead. The parking area is on the right side of the road and there is a sign marking it. Trailhead GPS coordinates are 46 06.336N 122 12.782W.

Key points:
0.1 Cave entrance.
0.6 The Meatball.
0.8 Crawl space at end of cave.

Ape Cave

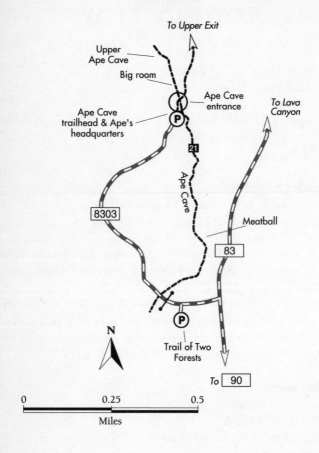

To Upper Exit

Upper Ape Cave

Big room

Ape Cave entrance

To Lava Canyon

Ape Cave trailhead & Ape's headquarters

P

21

Ape Cave

Meatball

8303

83

N

P

Trail of Two Forests

To 90

0   0.25   0.5
Miles

The hike: This is a very popular cave, so traffic may be heavy. The main hazard in this cave is the darkness. Two good sources of light are recommended for each person entering the cave. Because hiking this section of Ape Cave requires little or no use of the hands, a lantern makes a good light source. I personally like to wear a headlamp as well as carry a lantern. The cave floor is generally fairly smooth, but there are rocks lying on it that can be real shin busters and one spot where you must step down about a foot and a half. In one spot very tall hikers may have to duck for a low ceiling. The temperature inside the cave is about 42 degrees year round and there is some water dripping from the ceiling at times, so dress accordingly.

Leave the paved parking area and head north on the paved trail between Ape's Headquarters and the restroom. In 175 yards you will reach the main entrance to Ape Cave. Before entering the cave, stop and read the information signs in the gazebo. This information will help you to know what to look for in the cave.

Descend the steps and enter the cave. It is a good idea to stop at the top of the second set of steps and let your eyes adjust to the lack of light before climbing down to the cave floor. This is also the spot to turn on your headlamp and make sure your lantern is running. At the bottom of the second set of steps the upper and lower cave routes split. A sign here points you south into the lower cave.

About 150 yards into the lower cave, if you are walking close to the left wall as most hikers do here, there will be a step down of 1.5 feet. For most people this is the only place in the cave where you will want to use your hand for balance. Half a mile from the cave entrance, The Meatball comes into view overhead. The Meatball is the last and largest of several boulders stuck in an opening in the cave ceiling.

The cave divides into upper and lower passages 0.2 mile past The Meatball. Continue on a short distance in the lower passage. The passage quickly gets smaller and lower; soon you will be on your hands and knees. This is as far as most people go in the cave. If you crawl and slither any farther be very careful not to go too far and get stuck. Do not crawl into the last section if you are alone. A person who gets stuck here could easily die from hypothermia. Retracing your steps makes the return trip.

Options: Hike the trail to the upper exit of Upper Ape Cave.

11
TRAIL OF TWO FORESTS

Type of hike: Loop.
Total distance: 0.3 mile.
Elevation gain: Minimal.
Maps: The one on the signboard at the trailhead is more than adequate.
Starting Point: Trail of Two Forests Parking Area.

Finding the trailhead: Drive Interstate 5 to Exit 21 (21 miles north of Columbia River Bridge or approximately 150 miles south from Seattle) at Woodland. Then drive east on Washington 503 (which becomes WA 503 spur) for 27.5 miles to Cougar. From Cougar drive east on WA 503 spur (which becomes Forest Road 90 at the Skamania County line) for 6.8 miles to the junction with FR 83. Turns left (northwest) on FR 83 and follow it for 2 miles to FR 8303. Turn left again on FR 8303 and follow it 0.2 miles to the trailhead. A sign marks the parking area and trailhead on the left side of FR 8303.

Key points:
45 yards   Boardwalk starts at junction.
85 yards   Forest returns sign.
120 yards Cushions of life sign.
175 yards Path to The Crawl exit.
190 yards Tree molds sign.

Trail of Two Forests

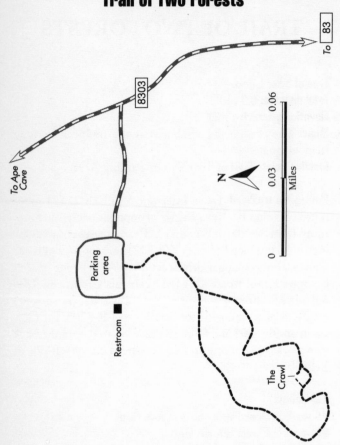

205 yards Rim of Rock sign.
220 yards Entrance to The Crawl.
260 yards Lava Log Dam sign.
360 yards The Tunnel sign.
425 yards Junction with paved trail back to parking area.

The hike: Leave the trailhead and walk south 45 yards on the paved, barrier-free trail to the junction and the beginning of the boardwalk. Bear left at the junction and go another 40 yards to the sign explaining the return of the forest after an eruption 2,000 years ago. Next, come to a sign that describes how moss breaks down the lava so that other plants can take root.

A bit farther along a paved path to the right leads 10 yards to the exit from The Crawl. The Crawl is a horizontal tree mold about 50 feet long and about 2.5 feet in diameter. It was formed when hot lava engulfed a fallen tree. The tree burned and rotted away after the lava solidified leaving a round hole through the rock. Read the Tree Molds signs just ahead for more information about this process.

The Crawl will probably be the high point of this hike if you have children along. The entrance for The Crawl is about 50 yards ahead on the trail. It can easily be seen across the lava flow, to your left, from the end of the side path. If you have small children it is best to leave an adult at the exit and send the children with another adult ahead to the entrance. This way the children can be talked through the short cave. You can see through the straight opening, so lights are not necessary. Be very careful at the entrance and exit since there is the possibility of falling from the metal steps to the rocks below.

When you are finished with The Crawl, continue another 40 yards past the entrance to a sign explaining a lava log dam. One hundred yards after passing the log dam, a lava tube cave can be seen to your right, out on the moss—covered lava flow. A short distance more brings you to the junction where you got on the boardwalk. Turn left, and walk the 45 yards back to the parking area on the paved trail.

Allow plenty of time to read the very informative signs along this trail. If you quietly hike this path very early in the morning, you may see one or more of the many cottontail rabbits that inhabit the area.

Options: Walk this barrier-free loop on the same trip that you hike Ape Cave.

12
PTARMIGAN TRAIL

Type of hike: Out and back.
Total distance: 4.6 miles.
Elevation gain: 1,050 feet.
Maps: MSHNVM. Mount St. Helens USGS quad covers the area but this trail is not shown.
Starting point: Climbers Bivouac Trailhead.

Finding the trailhead: Head north from Portland or south from Seattle on Interstate 5 to Exit 21 at Woodland, Washington (21 miles from the Columbia River Bridge or about 150 miles from Seattle). Drive east on Washington 503 (which becomes WA 503 spur, then Forest Road 90) for 34.3 miles, passing Cougar, to the junction with FR 83. Turn left on FR 83 and follow it for 3.1 miles north to the junction with FR 81. Turn left on FR 81 and drive northwest 1.6 miles to the junction with FR 830. Turn right and head northeast on FR 803 for 2.6 miles to Climbers Bivouac Trailhead. FR 830 is a gravel road. GPS coordinates are 46 08.799N 122 10.991W.

Key points:

2.1 Junction with Loowit Trail. GPS 46 09.865N 122 11.433W.
2.3 Trail ends and climbing route begins.

Ptarmigan Trail

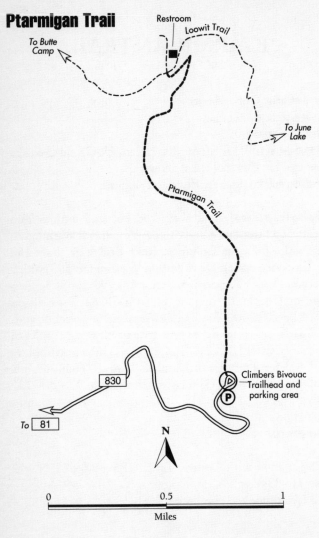

Restroom

Loowit Trail

To Butte Camp

To June Lake

Ptarmigan Trail

830

To 81

Climbers Bivouac Trailhead and parking area

N

0   0.5   1

Miles

The hike: The Ptarmigan Trail begins to climb gently to the north as it leaves the parking area at the Climbers Bivouac. The route is marked with blue diamond cross-country ski markers. The wide, well-maintained trail heads north through fir forest and huckleberry bushes. Avalanche lilies dot the ground between the bushes and trees. A sign marks the boundary of Mount St. Helens National Volcanic Monument 0.3 miles from the trailhead.

At 1.3 miles is the first good view of Mount St. Helens past the parking area. Now beargrass shares the openings with the huckleberries. The tread gets close to a lava flow 0.3 mile farther along. As you climb, Mount Hood and Mount Adams come into view to the south and east. Two miles from the trailhead the trail makes a switchback to the left. Reach the junction with the Loowit Trail 0.1 mile after passing the switchback, at 4,600 feet elevation.

Cross the Loowit Trail and hike on up through the timber. Just after passing the junction with the Loowit Trail a short path to the right leads to a restroom. The trail bears left and leaves the larger timber 0.2 miles from the Loowit Trail at about 4,750 feet elevation. The trail heads west for a short distance through the small alpine firs. This is where the trail ends and the climbing route begins.

Options: The Ptarmigan Trail is used as an approach trail for climbers ascending the Monitor Ridge Route to the summit of Mount St. Helens. If the summit is your goal, you must have a climbing permit. Hiking on Mount St. Helens above 4,800 feet elevation is not allowed without a climbing permit.

June Lake

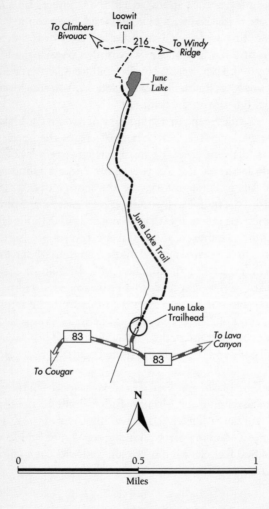

To Climbers
Bivouac

Loowit
Trail

216 → To Windy
Ridge

June
Lake

June Lake Trail

June Lake
Trailhead

83

83

To Cougar

To Lava
Canyon

N

0   0.5   1
Miles

13
JUNE LAKE

Type of hike: Out and back.
Total distance: 2.2 miles.
Elevation gain: 420 feet.
Maps: MSHNVM. Mount St. Helens USGS quad covers the area but does not show the trail.
Starting Point: June Lake Trailhead.

Finding the trailhead: From Portland, take Interstate 5 north to Exit 21 at Woodland, Washington; from Seattle, drive I-5 south to Exit 21 (approximately 150 miles). Then follow Washington 503 (which becomes WA 503 spur) east for 27.5 miles to Cougar. From Cougar drive east on WA 503 spur, (which becomes Forest Road 90) for 6.8 miles to the junction with FR 83. Turn left (north) on FR 83 and follow it 5.6 miles to the marked turnoff to June Lake Trailhead. The trailhead is a short distance north of FR 83 on a paved side road. Trailhead GPS coordinates are 46 08.237N 122 09.442W.

Key Points:
1.1 June Lake.

The hike: Leave the trailhead and head north on a trail marked with blue diamond cross-country ski markers. You are a few yards to the right of a creek as you begin your hike. As you ascend gently through the second-growth forest of fir and hemlock, glimpses of the smooth south slopes of Mount St. Helens appear ahead. The path winds up through the woods, sometimes close to the creek and sometimes a distance away.

A lava flow comes into view to the left across the creek, 0.8 mile from the trailhead. Here the view of the mountain really opens up. Soon you cross a tiny stream then climb over a small rise before descending a few feet to a sandy area. Once past the sandy area the trail climbs a few yards to a bridge over the outlet of June Lake. The lake is in view to the right only a few yards away.

Steep hills and cliffs surround June Lake, elevation 3,130 feet, on three sides. The hills next to the lake have never been logged, so beautiful old-growth forest remains around much of the shoreline. A waterfall plunges into the lake on the northeast side. Smaller falls enter the lake in a couple of other spots. The sandy beach next to the lake is a great spot to have lunch.

Options: The return trip is generally made by retracing your steps back to the June Lake Trailhead. A more interesting alternate hike can be done by climbing on up the June Lake Trail for 0.3 mile to the Loowit Trail. Turn left (west) on the Loowit Trail and follow it for 3.3 miles to the Ptarmigan Trail. Then turn left (south) again and descend the Ptarmigan Trail for 2.1 miles to the Climbers Bivouac Trailhead. This alternate return requires a car shuttle to the Climbers Bivouac Trailhead. See Hike 12 for information on this much longer and more difficult alternate return hike.

14
APE CANYON

Type of hike: Out and back.
Total distance: 9.6 miles.
Elevation gain: 1,340 feet.
Maps: MSHNVM. USGS Mount St. Helens and Smith Creek Butte quads cover the area but this trail is not shown.
Starting point: Ape Canyon Trailhead.

Finding the trailhead: From Seattle, drive south on Interstate 5 for approximately 150 miles to Woodland. From Portland take I-5 to Woodland. Take Exit 21 from I-5 and drive east on Washington 503 (which becomes WA 503 spur and then Forest Road 90) through Cougar. Turn left off FR 90, 34.8 miles east of I-5 (6.8 miles east of Cougar) onto Forest Road 83. Follow FR 83 for 11.5 miles to the Ape Canyon Trailhead. The signed trailhead is on the left side of the road. GPS coordinates at the trailhead are 46 09.917N 122 05.536W.

Key points:
2.6 Cross ridgeline.
4.7 Viewpoint of Ape Canyon.
4.8 Junction with Loowit Trail.

The hike: The Ape Canyon Trail climbs gently as it leaves the trailhead. After a short distance, the path turns right along the

Ape Canyon

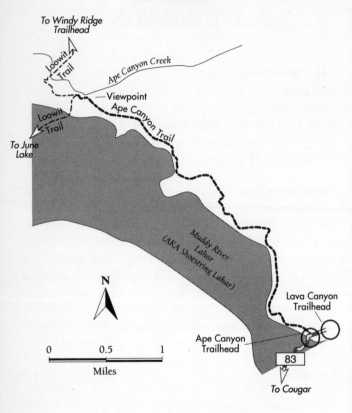

To Windy Ridge
Trailhead

Loowit
Trail

Ape Canyon Creek

Viewpoint
Ape Canyon Trail

Loowit
Trail

To June
Lake

Muddy River
Lahar
(AKA Shoestring Lahar)

N

0   0.5   1
Miles

Lava Canyon
Trailhead

Ape Canyon
Trailhead

83

To Cougar

bank of the Muddy River Lahar. Four-tenths of a mile from the trailhead the trail follows an abandoned roadbed for a short distance. Soon the route leads up a small, open ridge with great views. The path traverses off the left side of the ridge, through vine maple, alder and huckleberry bushes. You will continue to climb gently through the small forest until you are about 0.9 mile from the trailhead. Here the route enters larger timber, with some large old-growth Douglas-firs. Half a mile farther along the trail makes the first of five switchbacks and takes you up to a ridgeline. The path crosses the ridge 2.6 miles from the trailhead. The tread traverses a brushy area after crossing the ridge. Here both Mount Rainier and Mount Adams come into view.

Continuing to climb, the trail generally follows the ridge. The Blast Zone across Ape Canyon comes into view 3.5 miles from the trailhead. The path makes its way up the ridge for another 1.2 miles to the viewpoint of the gorge in upper Ape Canyon. Take the time to walk the short distance to the right of the trail to the viewpoint. If you have children with you be very careful at the viewpoint; the cliffs drop away below and the ground is not very stable. From the viewpoint the route heads west-northwest another 0.1 mile to the junction with the Loowit Trail, at 4,190 feet elevation.

The junction with the Loowit Trail is very near the timberline. Flowers cover much of the open area in July. Watch for a colony of whistle pigs (hoary marmots) that inhabit the upper part of Ape Canyon above the gorge.

Options: By turning right (north) on the Loowit Trail you can hike 6 miles across The Plains of Abraham to the Windy Ridge Viewpoint and Trailhead. However, hiking to Windy Ridge would require a long car shuttle. See Hike 17 for details.

15
LAVA CANYON

Type of hike: Out and back with shuttle and loop options.
Total distance: 6.0 miles; shuttle 3 miles; loop 1.4 miles.
Elevation loss: 1,130 feet; loop 300 feet.
Maps: MSHNVM. USGS Smith Creek Butte quad covers the area but the trail is not shown.
Starting point: Lava Canyon Trailhead.

Finding the trailhead: From Seattle, drive south on Interstate 5 for approximately 150 miles to Woodland. From Portland take I-5 north 21 miles to Woodland. Then take Exit 21 from I-5, and drive east on Washington 503 (which becomes WA 503 spur) through Cougar. WA 503 spur becomes Forest Road 90 east of Cougar at the Skamania County line. 34.8 miles east of I-5 (6.8 miles east of Cougar) turn left off of FR 90 onto FR 83. Follow FR 83 for 11.7 miles to the Lava Canyon Trailhead. GPS coordinates at the trailhead are 46 09.912N 122 05.286W.

To reach Lower Smith Creek Trailhead, where Lava Canyon Trail ends, head back toward FR 90 on FR 83 for 0.8 mile then turn left (southeast) on FR 8322. Follow FR 8322 for 4.8 miles to Lower Smith Creek Trailhead. FR 8322 is a rough, narrow, gravel road.

Lava Canyon

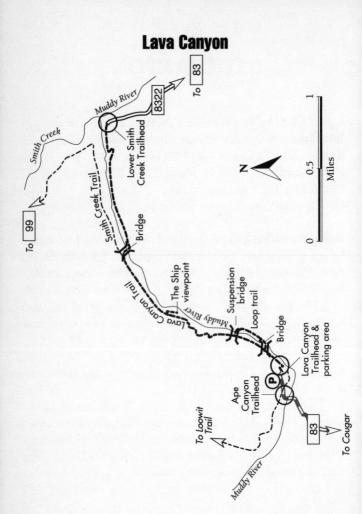

Key points:

0.3 Junction with Loop Trail, near end of the barrier-free trail.

0.7 Junction with Loop Trail at suspension bridge.

1.4 Ladder.

1.7 Junction with the trail to The Ship viewpoint.

2.0 Junction with Smith Creek Trail, new bridge.

3.0 Lower Smith Creek Trailhead. GPS 46 10.926N 122 03.302W.

The hike: The Loop is rough and slippery in spots. Below the Loop the trail is very rough, exposed and slippery in spots. The ladders, which must be descended to continue down to the Smith Creek Trail and to The Ship, can be slippery when wet. The trail to The Ship is also very difficult and exposed.

The paved trail leaves the south side of the parking area, descending gently. You will make a couple of switchbacks and pass some benches before reaching an interpretive viewpoint. The viewpoint is a wooden platform with a handrail and information sign. Past the viewpoint the trail continues to descend gently to the upper junction with the Loop Trail. A short distance ahead is the end of the barrier-free trail and another interpretive viewpoint.

The rough Loop Trail turns to the right (southeast) and drops to cross a bridge over the Muddy River. This alternate route then descends, sometimes steeply, for 0.5 mile to rejoin the main trail at the suspension bridge.

The main trail now becomes steeper and rougher as it works its way down from the upper junction with the Loop Trail. In 0.4 mile you will reach the lower junction with the

Loop Trail at the suspension bridge. The bridge is suspended over a narrow gorge; it sways and bounces as you walk across it. If you want to return from here, cross the bridge and climb back up the Loop Trail.

The suspension bridge is the turnaround point for the casual hiker. Below here, the trail is steep, very rough, and exposed in some places. To continue down, descend north and northeast from the suspension bridge, crossing a stream with a cable handrail. The route makes several switchbacks in the 0.7 mile to the ladder, passing wonderful falls and beautiful pools along the way. The 30-foot steel ladder allows the trail to drop over a cliff of basalt. The slippery-when-wet ladder must be descended to continue down. Once down the ladder the rough path heads down and crosses another stream to the junction with a side trail to The Ship viewpoint.

The side trail turns to the right (southeast) and climbs very steeply to The Ship viewpoint 0.2 mile away. The Ship is a large rock outcrop above the riverbed. The view from The Ship is well worth the effort it takes to get there, but the trail is very steep and exposed. There is another steel ladder on the path to The Ship viewpoint. Do not send children up the trail to The Ship viewpoint alone. Below the junction with the path to The Ship viewpoint, the Lava Canyon Trail continues down, crossing a couple more exposed spots.

Two miles from the Lava Canyon Trailhead is the new junction with the Smith Creek Trail. The Lava Canyon Trail used to continue another 0.9 mile east to the banks of Smith Creek where it met the Smith Creek Trail but now that lower

0.9 mile has become part of the Smith Creek Trail. At this junction, the Lava Canyon Trail turns to the right and crosses a bridge over the Muddy River (This bridge should be in place by early 1999). It then descends for 1 mile to the Lower Smith Creek Trailhead, making a couple of switchbacks along the way. The Lower Smith Creek Trailhead is at 1,700 feet elevation, 3 miles from the Lava Canyon Trailhead.

Options: The loop trail is an excellent option for a family hike. Retracing your steps can make the return from the Lower Smith Creek Trailhead or you can make a car shuttle.

Eastern Region
Access from Cougar, Washington

The eastern region of Mount St. Helens National Volcanic Monument is mostly within the Blast and Singe Zones caused by the 1980 eruption. Much of this region is covered with wildflowers between the broken stumps, blown-down trees, and beautiful silver snags.

As you start west up Forest Road 99 from Forest Road 25, you will drive through large old-growth forest. First you will reach Bear Meadows Trailhead where the hike to Ghost Lake (Hike 16) begins. Shortly after passing Bear Meadows you will begin to enter The Blast Zone. Mount St. Helens soon comes into view between the denuded trees.

Continuing on FR 99, you soon arrive at the junction with Forest Road 26. FR 26 bears right off FR 99 and leads to Norway Pass Trailhead and the trailheads along the upper Green River. The easiest access into the Mount Margaret Backcounty is from Norway Pass Trailhead. The Miner's Car Exhibit, which is the trailhead for Meta Lake (Hike 21) is located next to the junction of FR 99 and FR 26.

FR 99 soon bears to the southwest and passes Harmony Trailhead, the starting point for Harmony Trail (Hike 19), before reaching Windy Ridge Viewpoint and Trailhead at the end of the road. Windy Ridge Viewpoint is the trailhead for Hike 17 and 20, and offers the best view of the Mount St. Helens crater to be had on this side of the Monument.

16
GHOST LAKE

Type of hike: Out and back.
Total distance: 8 miles.
Elevation gain: 300 feet.
Maps: MSHNVM or Spirit Lake East USGS quad.
Starting point: Bear Meadows Viewpoint and Trailhead.

Finding the trailhead: Head north from Portland on Interstate 5 to Exit 21 (21 miles north of the Columbia River Bridge) at Woodland. Then drive east for 27.5 miles on Washington 503 (which becomes WA 503 spur) to Cougar. Continue east through Cougar on WA 503 spur (which becomes Forest Road 90 at the Skamania County line) for another 18.6 miles to the junction with FR 25. Bear left (nearly straight ahead) and head northeast on FR 25 for 24.3 miles to the junction with FR 99.

From Seattle, take I-5 south to Exit 133 at Tacoma, and then follow WA 7 for 55 miles to Morton. From Morton, drive east 17 miles to Randle. Turn right and take WA 131, which soon becomes FR 25, south for 20 miles to the junction with FR 99.

Turn right (west) on FR 99 and follow it for 4.5 miles to Bear Pass Trailhead. The trail leaves from the right side of the road across from the parking area. GPS coordinates at the trailhead are 46 18.799 N 122 02.167 W.

Ghost Lake

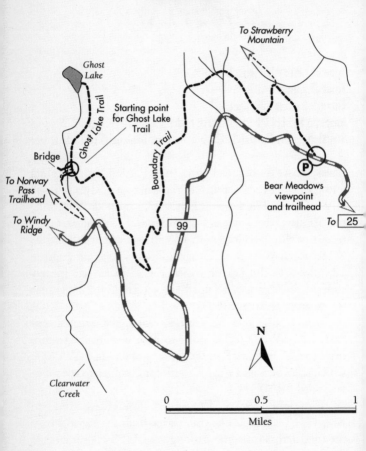

Ghost Lake

Ghost Lake Trail

Starting point for Ghost Lake Trail

Bridge

To Norway Pass Trailhead

To Windy Ridge

Boundary Trail

99

To Strawberry Mountain

P

Bear Meadows viewpoint and trailhead

To 25

Clearwater Creek

N

| 0 | 0.5 | 1 |

Miles

Key points:
0.6   Junction with Strawberry Mountain Trail.
3.3   Junction with Ghost Lake Trail.
4.0   Ghost Lake.

The hike: The pumice-covered Boundary Trail climbs through small timber intermingled with paintbrush and penstemon as it leaves the Bear Meadows Trailhead. Three hundred yards from the trailhead you will enter old growth forest of fir and hemlock. The path climbs gently but steadily for 0.6 mile to the junction with the Strawberry Mountain Trail, at 4,360 feet elevation. The Strawberry Mountain Trail turns to the right (northwest) and ascends Strawberry Mountain. Bear left at the junction and continue through the large timber. As you traverse the slope to the south, notice the avalanche lilies dotting the forest floor.

The route rounds the end of a ridge where you can spot FR 99 below. Mount St. Helens looms to the southwest through the trees. The tread crosses a small stream 1 mile from the trailhead. It then crosses a larger stream at the base of a stepped waterfall. Continue the traverse of this steep-sided hill, crossing a couple more small streams. In an opening on the slope, shooting stars, larkspur and paintbrush grow in profusion. Watch for a view of Mount Adams to your left.

The trail enters The Blast Zone 2 miles from Bear Meadows. The standing dead snags attest to the heat and power of the 1980 eruption. Huckleberries are plentiful here in August. You will make five switchbacks as you descend to a broken wooden bridge over a usually dry stream.

A short distance past the bridge is the unmarked junction with the Ghost Lake Trail. From the junction, 3.3 miles from Bear Meadows, Ghost Lake is 0.7 mile to the right.

From the unmarked junction with the Boundary Trail, the Ghost Lake Trail leads north. The path is right on the edge between the green forest on your left and the silver snags to your right. The green timber is a pocket of trees that were shielded by a hill and survived the 1980 eruption. As the route heads up the east side of Clearwater Creek it passes a small meadow. Soon you leave the large green trees behind and travel through dead snags and fallen timber. The forest is regenerating itself; young trees are growing up between the snags. Huckleberries cover the ground between the trees. The tread enters an area of pumice landslide debris 0.5 mile from the Boundary Trail. Here the path nearly disappears.

Turn left (west) on the pumice to reach the lakeshore. Mosquitoes can be bad at Ghost Lake so come prepared. Trout, some of them fairly good-sized, are plentiful in the lake.

Options: Taking the Strawberry Mountain Trail to the summit of Strawberry Mountain and back is a 4-mile side trip.

17
PLAINS OF ABRAHAM LOOP

Type of hike: Loop.
Total distance: 8.7 miles.
Elevation gain: 1,000 feet.
Maps: MSHNVM. Mount St. Helens and Spirit Lake West USGS quads cover the area but this trail is not shown.
Starting point: Windy Ridge Viewpoint and Trailhead.

Finding the trailhead: Head north from Portland on Interstate 5 to Exit 21 (21 miles north of the Columbia River Bridge) at Woodland. Drive east for 27.5 miles on Washington 503 (which becomes WA 503 spur) to Cougar. Continue east through Cougar on WA 503 spur (which becomes Forest Road 90 at the Skamania County line), for another 18.6 miles to the junction with FR 25. Bear left (nearly straight ahead) and head northeast on FR 25 for 24.3 miles to the junction with FR 99.

From Seattle, take I-5 south to Exit 133 then follow WA 7 for 55 miles to Morton. From Morton, drive east 17 miles to Randle on U.S. Highway 12. Turn right and take WA 131, which soon becomes FR 25, south for 20 miles to the junction with FR 99.

From the junction turn west on FR 99 and drive 15.8 miles to the trailhead. GPS coordinates 46 15.990N 122 08.200W.

Plains of Abraham Loop

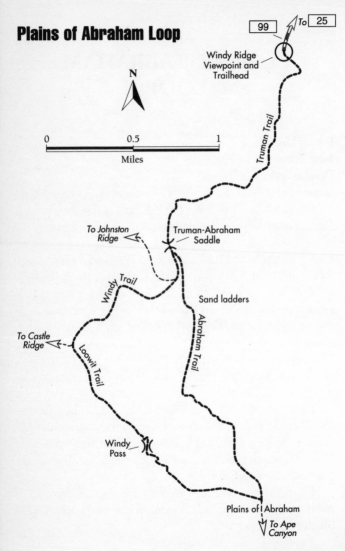

Key points:
1.7 Junction with Abraham Trail.
3.9 Junction with Loowit Trail on the Plains of Abraham.
5.0 Windy Pass.
6.0 Junction with Windy Trail.
6.8 Junction with Truman Trail.
7.0 Junction with Abraham Trail in Truman–Abraham Saddle.

The hike: The Truman Trail, which is really a closed section of FR 99 at this point, heads south from the Windy Ridge Viewpoint and Trailhead. The route travels along the east side of Windy Ridge through the severely blasted forest. Penstemon and paintbrush color the slopes between the alder and huckleberry bushes. Mount Adams is in view to the east across Smith Creek Canyon. About 1.5 miles from the trailhead, a wet spot on the right side of the trail produces a patch of Lewis monkeyflowers.

In the Truman–Abraham Saddle, at 4,160 feet elevation and 1.7 miles from the trailhead, the Abraham Trail bears left (southeast) off the Truman Trail. The path climbs a narrow pumice ridge with Smith Creek Canyon to the left and Mount St. Helens ahead to the right. In late July the flowers along this ridge are unrivaled. Penstemon and paintbrush nearly cover the slopes. The route climbs its first sand ladder 0.3 miles from the junction. A sand ladder is a series of wooden rungs held together with cables. The purpose of a sand ladder is to allow easier climbing and descending over steep loose soil. A little farther up you will climb another sand ladder and regain the ridgeline.

The route then follows the ridge to the south and climbs to a high point. Here the path flattens out for a short distance. Leopard lilies and columbines line the trail.

The route climbs a bit more then bears left off the ridgeline, 0.9 mile from Truman Trail. You will cross six draws in the next 0.7 mile. A couple of these draws may have water through midsummer. All of them are flower gardens in late July. The wetter draws grow stands of monkeyflowers. After crossing the sixth draw the Plains of Abraham come into view ahead.

The tread descends, then crosses a wash as it nears the plains. You will make a switchback as you climb out of the wash onto the desert-like plains. Few plants can withstand the rigors of this pumice desert, but a few penstemons seem to prosper and bloom.

The route crosses the plains heading south-southeast for 0.3 mile to the junction with the Loowit Trail. This junction is 3.9 miles from Windy Ridge Trailhead. It is about 1.6 miles straight ahead and across the plains to the south to the junction with Ape Canyon Trail.

To continue on the loop, turn right at the junction and hike west across the plains on the Loowit Trail. Ape and Nelson Glaciers hang to the mountain slopes ahead and above. As you get closer to the base of the mountain the path bears slightly to the right and crosses a couple of washes. This section of the Loowit Trail is marked with large cairns. In the washes the trail is rough and vague in spots. You will leave the plains and begin to climb toward Windy Pass 0.7 mile from the junction. The route climbs the south facing, penstemon-covered slope and makes a couple of switchbacks before reaching Windy Pass. This is a pumice slope and the path tends to slip away in places if it has not been recently maintained.

The pass, at 4,890 feet elevation and 5 miles from the trailhead, is the highest spot on this loop. At the pass Spirit Lake comes into view to the north. The trail descends off the pass, making four switchbacks as it drops. It then descends a gully that may be snow-filled through July. Leaving the gully the tread traverses northwest, in and out of a couple more washes and past a small waterfall before it reaches the junction with Windy Trail.

The junction with the Windy Trail is 6.0 miles from the Windy Ridge Viewpoint and Trailhead. As of late summer 1998 the Loowit Trail is closed from this junction, 4 miles west, to Studebaker Ridge. This section of the Loowit Trail may be replaced in 1999, making an around-the-mountain hike possible again. The junction of the Windy and Loowit Trails is very close to the pre-eruption site of Timberline Campground. Before the 1980 eruption, the most popular climbing routes to the summit of Mount St. Helens started here at the end of a paved road. Nothing remains of the campground today.

Turn right on the Windy Trail and hike northeast. You will descend gently through the mounds of pumice. The path descends into a large wash 0.6 mile after leaving the Loowit Trail. Another 0.2 mile brings you to the junction with the Truman Trail. Turn right on the Truman Trail and climb gently up the roadbed for 0.3 mile to the junction with the Abraham Trail in the Truman–Abraham Saddle to complete the loop. Retrace your steps north on the Truman Trail for 1.7 miles to the Windy Ridge Trailhead.

Options: Hike south from the junction of the Abraham and Loowit Trails, across the Plains of Abraham to the Ape Canyon Trail, then from there along the Ape Canyon Trail to the Ape Canyon Trailhead; this makes a great day hike. The car shuttle to the Ape Canyon Trailhead is, however, quite long. See Hike 14 for a description of the Ape Canyon Trail.

18
INDEPENDENCE LOOP

Type of hike: Loop.
Total distance: 6.7 miles.
Elevation gain: 860 feet.
Maps: MSHNVM or USGS Spirit Lake East quad.
Starting point: Independence Pass Trailhead.

Finding the trailhead: Head north from Portland on Interstate 5 to Exit 21 (21 miles north of the Columbia River Bridge) at Woodland. Drive east for 27.5 miles on Washington 503 (which becomes WA 503 spur) to Cougar. Continue east through Cougar on WA 503 spur (which becomes Forest Road 90 at the Skamania County line), for another 18.6 miles to the junction with FR 25. Bear left (nearly straight ahead) and head northeast on FR 25 for 24.3 miles to the junction with FR 99.

From Seattle take I-5 south to Exit 133 at Tacoma, and then follow WA 7 for 55 miles to Morton. From Morton drive east 17 miles to Randle. Turn right and take WA 131 (which becomes FR 25) on US Highway 12 for 20 miles to the junction with FR 99.

Turn west on FR 99 and follow it 11.9 miles to the Independence Pass Trailhead. The trailhead is on the right (west) side of FR 99. GPS coordinates at the trailhead are 46 16.916N 122 05.798W.

Independence Loop

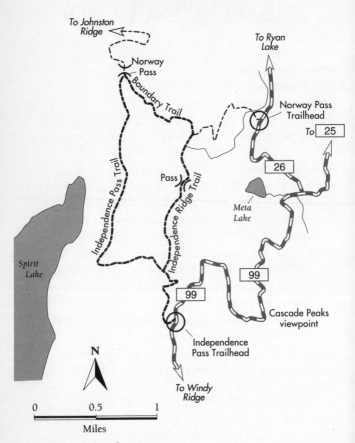

To Johnston Ridge

Norway Pass

Boundary Trail

To Ryan Lake

Norway Pass Trailhead

To 25

26

Independence Pass Trail

Pass

Independence Ridge Trail

Meta Lake

Spirit Lake

99

99

Cascade Peaks viewpoint

Independence Pass Trailhead

N

To Windy Ridge

0   0.5   1

Miles

Key points:

0.9 Junction with Independence Ridge Trail, GPS 46 17.396N 122 05.997W.
3.5 Norway Pass.
4.5 Junction with Independence Ridge Trail.
5.8 Junction with Independence Pass Trail.

The hike: As it leaves the trailhead the route climbs 30 steps, then makes a couple of switchbacks as it heads west to the ridgeline. Once you reach the ridge, Spirit Lake comes into view. From the ridge you can see Mount Hood far to the south and to the left of the blasted-out remains of Mount St. Helens. The ridge is covered with blown-down timber; scattered small firs and huckleberry bushes growing between the logs. The berries are ripe in late August.

The path turns right along the ridge and heads north through stands of fireweed and other flowers. The tread makes a couple more switchbacks 0.5 mile from the trailhead. It then begins to traverse a southwest-facing slope. Along this slope grow columbine and beargrass. Another 0.4 mile brings you to the junction with the Independence Ridge Trail on the side of a little valley. The Independence Ridge Trail turns to the right (northeast). The USGS map shows this junction incorrectly.

Bear left at the junction and follow the Independence Pass Trail. You will descend a few feet and cross the tiny valley. Through midsummer there is usually a spring in the bottom of the valley a few yards below the trail to the south. Leaving the valley the route climbs slightly to the west. Soon it descends and turns north along a steep slope above Spirit Lake.

The route passes beneath some cliffs 0.9 mile after leaving the junction with the Independence Ridge Trail. Look for pinnacles of rock below the trail as you pass the cliffs. The tread soon begins to climb and makes a couple of switchbacks. Then it winds up through a saddle.

Past the saddle the path traverses the west-facing slope, and Mount Rainier comes into view. In the shaded, damper spots along this slope a few avalanche lilies manage to survive, and bloom in early July. There is a viewpoint a few yards to the right of the trail 3.4 miles from the trailhead where you can view Mount Adams to the east. Descend the last 0.1 mile to Norway Pass and the junction with Boundary Trail, at 4,520 feet elevation.

Turn right at the junction and traverse a north-facing slope through clusters of mountain ash and huckleberries. You will cut back into a gully, cross a ridgeline and then descend to the junction with the Independence Ridge Trail 1 mile from Norway Pass. From this junction it is 1.1 miles to the left (east) to the Norway Pass Trailhead.

At the signed junction with the Independence Ridge Trail, turn right. The Independence Ridge Trail climbs gradually and southward. Meta Lake sits below and to the east, while Mount Adams rises above the green hills in the distance. Columbines, lupine, asters, bluebells, and leopard lilies cover the more open slopes. The vegetation on this slope is as lush as any within The Blast Zone.

The route reaches a pass 0.5 mile from the junction. At the pass, 4,670 feet above sea level, the slope becomes drier and the vegetation less dense. Beyond the pass the path crosses a large gully, traverses a slope, crosses several small gullies to another ridgeline 0.5 mile further. Paintbrush and penstemon color this slope. The tread follows the ridge for a short distance and then bears slightly to the right. Then you descend through short silvered snags, young firs and fireweed to the junction with Independence Pass Trail. This junction, which is shown incorrectly on the USGS map, is 1.3 miles from the junction with Boundary Trail and 5.8 miles into the loop.

Turn left (southeast) and retrace your steps back 0.9 miles to the Independence Pass Trailhead

Options: The hike can be shortened by 1.2 miles by descending the Boundary Trail to the Norway Pass Trailhead. Doing this requires a car shuttle between the trailheads.

Harmony Trail

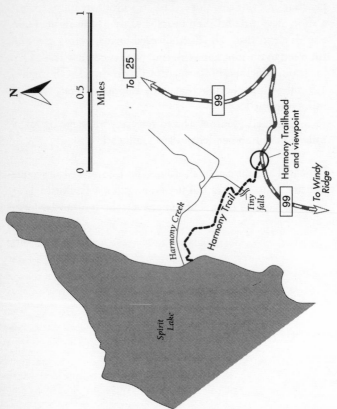

N

Miles

0   0.5   1

To 25

99

Harmony Creek

Spirit Lake

Harmony Trail

Tiny falls

Harmony Trailhead and viewpoint

99

To Windy Ridge

19
HARMONY TRAIL

Type of hike: Out and back.
Total distance: 2.4 miles.
Elevation Loss: 640 feet.
Maps: MSHNVM or Spirit Lake East USGS quad.
Starting point: Harmony Viewpoint and Trailhead.

Finding the trail: From Portland drive north on Interstate 5 to Exit 21 at Woodland, Washington. Follow Washington 503 (which becomes WA 503 spur) for 27.5 miles east to Cougar. From Cougar, drive east on WA 503 spur (which becomes FR 90) for 18.6 miles to the junction with FR 25. At the junction, FR 25 goes straight ahead (northeast). Follow FR 25 north for 24.3 miles to the junction with FR 99.

From Seattle take I-5 south to Exit 133, and then follow WA 7 for 55 miles to Morton. From Morton drive east, on U.S. Highway 12 for 17 miles to Randle. Turn right and take WA 131 (which becomes FR 25) south for 20 miles to the junction with FR 99.

Turn west on FR 99 and drive 13.5 miles to the Harmony Trailhead. There is a sign marking the trailhead and viewpoint. GPS coordinates 46 15.499N 122 07.027W.

Key points:
0.4 Tiny waterfall.
1.2 Spirit Lake.

The hike: The Harmony Trail immediately starts to descend from the trailhead. This north-facing slope is covered with low brush and blown-down logs. In a few yards the trail enters the restricted area as it begins a descending traverse to the west. In the restricted area, hikers may not leave the trail or camp. After descending the traverse for 0.2 mile, the trail makes a switchback to the right. It then turns left to continue its moderate descent. You will pass a tiny waterfall 300 yards farther along. Cross the tiny stream below the falls and then pass beneath an under-cut rock face. On the far side of the face is another tiny falls and stream. These streams may be dried up by midsummer.

The tread makes a switchback to the right 250 yards after passing the tiny waterfalls. The trail then descends a short distance and leaves the north-facing slope you have been on since leaving the trailhead. The vegetation becomes more sparse as you leave the slope. Make a turn to the left and head west again toward the lake following a line of posts across the pumice flats. The trail descends again 0.3 mile farther along. It soon makes a couple more switchbacks as it comes alongside Harmony Creek. This rushing stream has several small waterfalls. Shortly after the trail comes to an end close to the log-strewn shore of Spirit Lake, at 3,410 feet elevation.

The end of the trail offers an excellent view of Mount St. Helens over the lake. Often the mountain reflects in the still water. Harmony Falls Lodge once sat next to the lakeshore, a short distance west of the end of the trail. The site of the old lodge is below the present lake level, which is about 200 feet higher than it was before the May 1980 eruption. Watch for elk all along this trail.

Options: The return trip is made via the same route.

Independence Pass Trail
(South Segment)

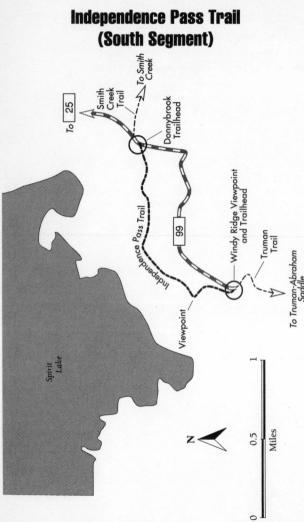

To Smith Creek

Smith Creek Trail

To 25

Donnybrook Trailhead

99

Windy Ridge Viewpoint and Trailhead

Truman Trail

Independence Pass Trail

Viewpoint

To Truman-Abraham Saddle

Spirit Lake

N

0   0.5   1
Miles

20
INDEPENDENCE PASS
(SOUTH SEGMENT)

Type of hike: Shuttle or out and back.
Total distance: 1.4 miles.
Elevation gain: 520 feet.
Maps: MSHNVM. Spirit Lake West and Spirit Lake East USGS quads cover the area but this trail is not shown.
Starting point: Windy Ridge Viewpoint and Trailhead.

Finding the trailhead: Head north from Portland on Interstate 5 to Exit 21 (21 miles north of the Columbia River Bridge) at Woodland. Drive east for 27.5 miles on Washington 503 (which becomes WA 503 spur) to Cougar. Continue east through Cougar on WA 503 spur (which becomes Forest Road 90 at the Skamania County line) for another 18.6 miles to the junction with FR 25. Bear left (nearly straight ahead) and head northeast on FR 25 for 24.3 miles to the junction with FR 99.

From Seattle, take I-5 south to Exit 133 in Tacoma, and then follow WA 7 for 55 miles to Morton. Turn left at the south edge of Morton and drive east for 17 miles to Randle on U.S. Highway 12. Turn right and take WA 131 (which becomes FR 25) south for 20 miles to the junction with FR 99.

Turn right (west) on FR 99 and drive 15.8 miles to the Windy Ridge Viewpoint and Trailhead. This segment of the Independence Pass Trail starts next to the rest rooms at the north end of the parking area. GPS coordinates 46 15.990N 122 08.200W.

Key points:
0.2   Viewpoint.
1.4   Donnybrook Viewpoint.

The hike: Originally the first 0.2 mile of this trail was a true sand ladder — a series of wooden rungs held together with cables which allow easier climbing and descending over steep, loose soil. Now 8 rock and 428 wooden steps replace the old sand ladder.

Climb the steps and then bear left to the viewpoint at 4,230 feet elevation on the pumice-covered slope. Take some time here to admire nature's violent handiwork. Look into the crater and see what was once the inside of a mountain. Spirit Lake, with its thousands of floating logs, is below. To the west Johnston Ridge Observatory sits perched atop Johnston Ridge. At this viewpoint, 0.2 mile from the parking area, the majority of tourists turn around.

A sign near the viewpoint, "Rd.99, 1 1/4 miles" points to the northeast. Follow the trail past the sign. Mount Margaret and Mount Rainier come into view, while penstemon dots the landscape between the downed logs. These flowers bloom through July. As you get farther along into a slightly more protected area, paintbrush, fireweed, elderberries and huckleberries join the penstemon.

The path rounds a ridgeline 0.6 mile from the trailhead. Here you begin to traverse east along a north-facing slope.

The vegetation becomes much lusher on this hillside. Columbine and lupine bloom here in July. The route passes beneath cliffs 0.3 mile into the traverse. It then rounds another ridge and continues east. The path then descends gently, through the silvered snags, alder brush and fireweed to the Donnybrook Viewpoint and Trailhead on FR 99.

Options: A short (5 minutes or less) car shuttle can be made between the two trailheads or you can just walk the road back to Windy Ridge Viewpoint.

Meta Lake Trail

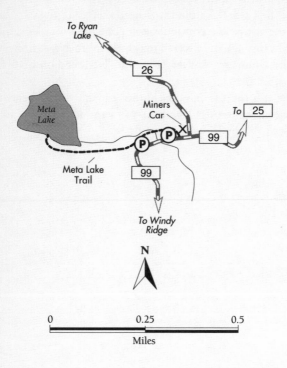

21
META LAKE

Type of hike: Out and back.
Total distance: 0.6 mile.
Elevation gain: Minimal.
Maps: None needed, Spirit Lake East USGS quad.
Starting point: Miners Car Exhibit site.

Finding the trailhead: Head north from Portland on Interstate 5 to Exit 21 (21 miles north of the Columbia River Bridge) at Woodland. Drive east for 27.5 miles on Washington 503 (which becomes WA 503 spur) to Cougar. Continue east through Cougar on WA 503 spur (which becomes Forest Road 90 at the Skamania County line) for another 18.6 miles to the junction with FR 25. Bear left (nearly straight ahead) and head northeast on FR 25 for 24.3 miles to the junction with FR 99.

From Seattle take I-5 south to Exit 133 at Tacoma, then follow WA 7 for 55 miles to Morton. From Morton, drive east on U.S. Highway 12 for 17 miles to Randle. Turn right and take WA 131 (which becomes FR 25) south for 20 miles to the junction with FR 99.

Turn west on FR 99 and drive 8.8 miles to the junction with FR 26, and the Miners Car Exhibit site. GPS coordinates 46 17.743N 122 04.507W.

Key points:
0.0 Miners Car Exhibit.
0.1 Meta Lake parking area.
0.3 Meta Lake.

The trail: Take a few minutes to check out the Miners Car Exhibit and imagine what it must have been like to have been here on May 18, 1980 when the volcano blew. From the Miners Car Exhibit, the paved trail parallels FR 99 for a couple hundred yards southwest to the Meta Lake parking area. Fireweed lines this section of trail along a sluggish stream. At the parking area the trail bears right—away from the road—and is no longer paved. The tread winds its way through the small fir trees and fireweed from the parking area to the lake. Along the way, stop and read the interpretive sign about "Survivors".

At the lake, 0.3 mile from where you started, another "Survivors" sign explains how frogs and brook trout survived the blast and ash under a covering of snow and ice.

Options: Return is made via the same trail.

22
RYAN LAKE LOOP

Type of hike: Loop.
Total distance: 0.6 mile.
Elevation gain: Minimal.
Maps: MSHNVM or Spirit Lake East USGS quad. No map
is really needed to follow this short, well-maintained loop.
Starting point: Ryan Lake Parking Area.

Finding the trailhead: Head north from Portland on Interstate
5 to Exit 21 (21 miles north of the Columbia River Bridge)
at Woodland. Drive east for 27.5 miles on Washington 503
(which becomes WA 503 spur) to Cougar. Continue east
through Cougar on WA 503 spur (which becomes Forest
Road 90 at the Skamania County line), for another 18.6
miles to the junction with FR 25. Bear left (nearly straight
ahead) and head northeast on FR 25 for 24.3 miles to the
junction with FR 99.

From Seattle take I-5 south to Exit 133 at Tacoma, and
then follow WA 7 for 55 miles to Morton. From Morton
drive east for 17 miles on U.S. Highway 12 to Randle. Turn
right and take WA 131 (which becomes FR 25) south for
20 miles to the junction with FR 99.

Turn right and head west on FR 99 for 8.8 miles to the
junction with FR 26. Turn right on FR 26 and drive 5 miles
to Ryan Lake Parking Area. The parking area is on the left

Ryan Lake Loop

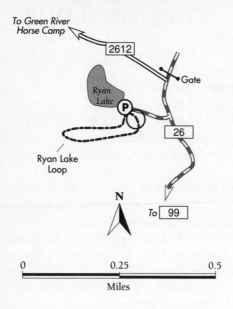

(west) side of the road. A restroom is available at the parking area, but there are no other facilities.

Key points:
0.3 Bench.
0.6 Return to parking area.

The hike: The "Red Zone"—a 10-mile wide circle drawn around Mount St. Helens in the months preceding the 1980 eruption that was supposed to be the danger area—did not extend as far as Ryan Lake. There were three campers here when the mountain blew; all three died in the hot gases and ash cloud that reached the lake shortly after 8:30 a.m. on May 18, 1980.

The Ryan Lake Loop Trail leaves from the south side of the parking area. You wind and switchback up through the young forest for 150 yards. The path then turns west, leaving the young trees for a slope covered with silver snags and blown-down timber. Paintbrush line the trail as you pass beneath some fallen logs. Hike through a few more small trees and reach the rounded ridgeline. Between the snags, Ryan Lake sparkles below.

Some hikers will welcome a resting bench 0.3 mile from the parking area. Stop and read the interpretive sign next to the bench. The bench is at the high point of the trail, so from here the tread begins to descend. As you drop gently through the young Douglas-fir woods you will pass more interpretive signs. Take the time to stop and read them and learn more about the regenerating forest. The route returns to the parking area 0.6 mile after leaving it.

Options: You may want to walk down to the shore of Ryan Lake from the parking area. At present there are no fish in Ryan Lake.

Along Forest Road 25

Forest Road 25 parallels the eastern boundary of Mount St. Helens Volcanic Mounument and is the main access to many points of interest. Driving south from Randle you will reach the Woods Creek Information Station in 5.7 miles.

Across FR 25 from the information station is the trailhead for Hike 25 Woods Creek Watchable Wildlife Loop. The easy figure-eight loop explores wet lands and old-growth forest.

Farther south, 19.5 miles from Randle, is the trailhead for Hike 24 to beautiful Iron Creek Falls. Just past Iron Creek Falls Trailhead is the junction with FR 99. FR 99 climbs west to Windy Ridge with its viewpoints and trailheads.

Another 21.5 miles south is the trailhead for Cedar Flats Nature Trail (Hike 23). Cedar Flats Nature Trail is a short hike through huge old-growth forest. After pasing Cedar Flats Trailhead it's only 3.6 miles farther south to the junction with FR 90.

23
CEDAR FLATS NATURE TRAIL LOOP

Type of hike: Loop.
Total distance: 0.9 mile.
Elevation loss: Minimal.
Maps: Cedar Flats USGS quad.
Starting Point: Cedar Flats Trailhead.

Finding the trailhead: Head north from Portland on Interstate 5 to Exit 21 (21 miles north of the Columbia River Bridge) at Woodland. Drive east for 27.5 miles on Washington 503 (which becomes WA 503 spur) to Cougar. Continue east through Cougar on WA 503 spur (which becomes Forest Road 90 at the Skamania County line) for another 18.6 miles to the junction with FR 25. Bear left (nearly straight ahead) and head northeast on FR 25 for 3.6 miles to Cedar Flats Trailhead.

From Seattle, take I-5 south to Exit 133 at Tacoma, then follow WA 7 for 55 miles to Morton. From Morton, drive east on U.S. Highway 12 for 17 miles to Randle. Turn right and take WA 131, then FR 25 south for 41 miles to the Cedar Flats Trailhead; it is on the east side of the road. GPS coordinates at the trailhead are 46 06.729N 122 01.019W.

Cedar Flats Nature Trail

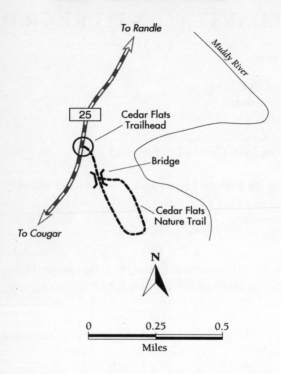

To Randle

Muddy River

25

Cedar Flats
Trailhead

Bridge

Cedar Flats
Nature Trail

To Cougar

N

0	0.25	0.5
Miles

Key points:

0.1 Wooden bridge and trail forks.

0.6 Viewpoint overlooking Muddy River.

The hike: Descending a few feet from the east side of the parking area, the Cedar Flats Nature Trail enters old-growth forest. The broad trail passes an interpretive sign and reaches a wooden bridge 0.1 mile from the trailhead. In the spring, when the new leaves are just out on the understory of vine maple, the sudued green light that filters down through the canopy makes these deep woods especially beautiful. Just past the bridge, the trail forks.

Bear right at the fork and continue along the well-maintained trail. You will pass some large cedar trees and in a few yards there will be two very large Douglas-firs to the left of the trail. This seems to be a favorite picture taking spot, as there is a path to the base of the largest tree.

The trail reaches the high bank of Muddy River 0.4 mile farther along, after passing many more large trees. A lahar flowed down the Muddy River during the 1980 eruption. The evidence of the deluge is still present in the form of logs and stumps scattered along the river bottom. The trail follows the riverbank for a couple hundred yards to a viewpoint with a short rail fence. At the viewpoint, the route turns away from the river and heads back through the woods. In about 300 yards you will reach the fork in the trail next to the bridge. Turn right and walk the last 0.1 mile back to the trailhead.

Options: Take your time and enjoy the old-growth forest.

Iron Creek Falls

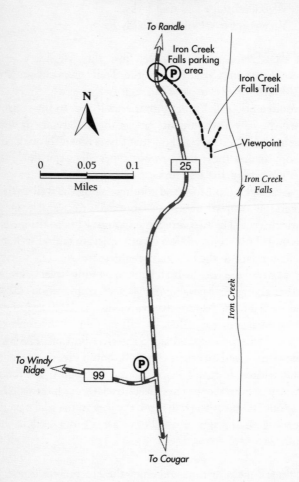

To Randle

Iron Creek
Falls parking
area

Iron Creek
Falls Trail

Viewpoint

Iron Creek
Falls

N

| 0 | 0.05 | 0.1 |
Miles

25

Iron Creek

To Windy
Ridge

99

To Cougar

24
IRON CREEK FALLS

Type of hike: Out and back.
Total distance: 0.2 mile.
Elevation loss: Minimal.
Maps: None needed.
Starting point: Iron Creek Falls Parking Area and Trailhead.

Finding the trailhead: Head north from Portland on Interstate 5 to Exit 21 (21 miles north of the Columbia River Bridge) at Woodland. Drive east for 27.5 miles on Washington 503 (which becomes WA 503 spur) to Cougar. Continue east through Cougar on WA 503 spur (which becomes FR 90 at the Skamania County line) for another 18.6 miles to the junction with FR 25. Bear left (nearly straight ahead) and head northeast on FR 25 for 24.8 miles to the trailhead.

From Seattle, take I-5 south to Exit 133 at Tacoma then follow WA 7 for 55 miles to Morton. From Morton drive east on U.S. Highway 12 for 17 miles to Randle. Turn right and take WA 131 (which becomes FR 25) south for 19.5 miles to the trailhead. The parking area is on the east side of FR 25.

Key points:
0.1 Iron Creek Falls Viewpoint.

The hike: A few yards from the trailhead you will start to descend the first of 58 wooden steps that take you to a switchback. Hemlock and fir line this path along a moss-covered slope. At the switchback, turn right and walk 30 yards to a viewpoint to look at Iron Creek Falls. Past the switchback, there are 16 more wooden steps and then a long step down to the creek bed. Walk up the creek bed 40 yards to get close to the falls. Iron Creek Falls drops over an undercut cliff and splashes with a roar into a beautiful pool at its base. As you climb the steps back to the parking area watch for the tiny white flowers that hug the side of the trail.

Options: Sit on the rocks and admire the falls.

25
WOODS CREEK WATCHABLE WILDLIFE LOOP

Type of hike: Loop.
Total distance: 2.4 miles.
Elevation gain: Minimal.
Maps: The one in this book or in pamphlet at trailhead.
Starting point: Woods Creek Trailhead and Picnic Area.

Finding the trailhead: Head north from Portland on Interstate 5 to Exit 21 (21 miles north of the Columbia River Bridge) at Woodland. Drive east for 27.5 miles on Washington 503 (which becomes WA 503 spur) to Cougar. Continue east through Cougar on WA 503 spur (which becomes Forest Road 90 at the Skamania County line), for another 18.6 miles to the junction with FR 25. Bear left (nearly straight ahead) and head northeast on FR 25 for 36.6 miles to Woods Creek Information Station.

From Seattle take I-5 south to Exit 133 at Tacoma, and then follow WA 7 for 55 miles to Morton. From Morton drive east on U.S. Highway 12 for 17 miles to Randle . Turn right at Randle and take WA 131 (which becomes FR 25) south for 5.7 miles to the Woods Creek Information Station.

The trailhead is on the east side of FR 25, across from the Information Station. GPS coordinates are 46 27.668N 121 57.574W.

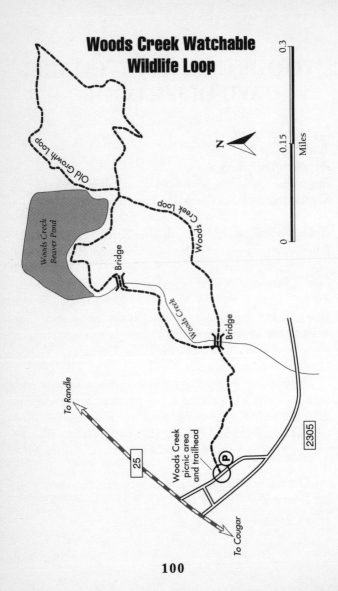

Woods Creek Watchable Wildlife Loop

Old Growth Loop

Woods Creek Beaver Pond

Bridge

Woods Creek Loop

Woods Creek

Bridge

N

0   0.15   0.3
Miles

To Randle

25

Woods Creek picnic area and trailhead

P

To Cougar

2305

100

Key points:

0.3   Junction with Woods Creek Loop.
0.8   Junction with Old Growth Loop.
2.1   Junction with Woods Creek Loop.
2.4   Picnic area.

The hike: This figure-eight loop hike is an excellent one for small children with adult supervision. As you leave the parking area pick up one of the pamphlets covering the Woods Creek Watchable Wildlife Interpretive Trail. A dispenser for the pamphlets and a donation box are located on the signboard next to the trailhead.

The four-foot-wide gravel tread heads east from the parking area through dense second-growth forest. Fir, bigleaf maple, and red cedar trees furnish the canopy. Beneath these big, moss-hung trees grows vine maple. Ferns and moss cover the ground. Soon after leaving the trailhead you will want to stop and read the first interpretive sign about deer tracks, some of which you may have already seen along the trail. After 0.3 mile you will reach a trail junction. At the junction there is a clearing and marsh next to the trail, as well as a bench and sign about elk tracks.

Turn left at the junction and hike northwest along the sluggish Woods Creek. Foxglove and blackberries line the creek, as do nettles. After passing another bench and sign about hare tracks you will cross a wooden bridge over Woods Creek. One-tenth of a mile farther along is a lookout porch to the left of the trail. The porch overlooks Woods Creek Beaver Pond. Just past the porch are another bench and a sign describing raccoon tracks.

Soon the junction with the Old Growth Loop Trail is reached. Turn left and then quickly turn right at another junction a few yards away. The Old Growth Loop climbs gently making a couple of switchbacks as it enters the larger trees of the old growth forest. Four-tenths of a mile into the Old Growth Loop you will find another bench and a sign about martin tracks. This bench is at the highest point of the hike. From here the trail descends, making another switchback and travels back to the junction with the Woods Creek Loop. At this junction first turn right then left

Once back on the Woods Creek Loop, the path heads east, then south, passing yet another bench and a sign about coyote tracks. Before long, after crossing a wooden bridge, you will reach another junction. This junction is the first one you came to when you began this hike. Turn left at the junction and hike the remaining 0.3 mile back to the trailhead.

Options: For a shorter hike, omit the Old Growth Loop.

About the Author

Fred Barstad grew up in Oregon's Willamette Valley and developed an interest in the Cascade Mountains at an early age. With his parents he hiked and fished extensively in the range, mostly between Mount Hood and Mount Jefferson in Oregon. The high volcanic peaks of the Cascades were always of special interest to him.

By the time Fred was a teenager in the 1960's this interest had become an addiction for the high and remote country. Fred has climbed most of the Cascades Volcanoes in Washington and Oregon, some of them many times. He climbed Mount St Helens 11 times before the 1980 eruption and a couple of times since. He has also climbed Mount McKinley in Alaska, Aconcagua in Argentina and Popocatepetl, Citlaltepetl and Iztaccihuatl in Mexico.

Fred now lives in Enterprise, Oregon at the base of the Wallowa Mountains. This is his fourth guidebook for Falcon Press, and he intends to write several more. He devotes his time to hiking, climbing, skiing, and snow-shoeing when not working on a book.

FALCON GUIDES ® Leading the Way™

LEAVE NO TRACE
by Will Harmon
The concept of "leave no trace" seems simple, but it is actually fairly complicated. This handy quick-reference guidebook is written to help the outdoor enthusiast make decisions necessary to protect the natural landscape and still have an enjoyable wilderness experience. Part of the proceeds go to continue leave-no-trace education efforts. The Official Manual of American Hiking Society.

BEAR AWARE
by Bill Schneider
Hiking in bear country can be very safe if hikers follow the guidelines summarized in this small, "packable" book. Extensively reviewed by bear experts, the book contains the latest information on the intriguing science of bear-human interactions. *Bear Aware* can not only make your hike safer, but it can help you avoid the fear of bears that can take the edge off your trip.

MOUNTAIN LION ALERT
By Steve Torres
Recent mountain lion attacks have received national attention. Although infrequent, these and other lion attacks raise concern for public safety. *Mountain Lion Alert* contains helpful advice for mountain bikers, trail runners, horse riders, pet owners, and suburban landowners on how to reduce the chances of mountain lion-human conflicts.

Also Available:
Avalanche Aware, Backpacking Tips, Leave No Trace,
Reading Weather, Route Finding, Wilderness First Aid,
Wilderness Survival, Climbing Safely, Desert Hiking Tips,
Hiking with Dogs, Using GPS, Wild Country Companion

To order these titles check with your local bookseller or
call FALCON® at 1-800-582-2665.
www.FalconOutdoors.com

FALCON GUIDES® Leading the Way™

All books in this popular series are regularly updated with accurate information on access, side trips, & safety.

HIKING GUIDES

Best Hikes Along the Continental Divide
Hiking Alaska
Hiking Arizona
Hiking Arizona's Cactus Country
Hiking the Beartooths
Hiking Big Bend National Park
Hiking the Bob Marshall Country
Hiking California
Hiking California's Desert Parks
Hiking Carlsbad Caverns & Guadalupe Mtns.
  National Parks
Hiking Colorado
Hiking Colorado, Vol. II
Hiking Colorado's Summits
Hiking Colorado's Weminuche Wilderness
Hiking the Columbia River Gorge
Hiking Florida
Hiking Georgia
Hiking Glacier/Waterton Lakes
Hiking Grand Canyon National Park
Hiking Grand Staircase-Escalante
Hiking Grand Teton National Park
Hiking Great Basin
Hiking Hot Springs in the Pacific NW
Hiking Idaho
Hiking Maine
Hiking Michigan
Hiking Minnesota
Hiking Montana
Hiking Mount Rainier National Park
Hiking Mount St. Helens
Hiking Nevada
Hiking New Hampshire
Hiking New Mexico
Hiking New York
Hiking North Carolina
Hiking North Cascades
Hiking Northern Arizona
Hiking Olympic National Park
Hiking Oregon

Hiking Oregon's Eagle Cap Wilderness
Hiking Oregon's Mt Hood/Badger Creek
Hiking Oregon's Three Sisters Country
Hiking Pennsylvania
Hiking Shenandoah National Park
Hiking the Sierra Nevada
Hiking South Carolina
Hiking South Dakota's Black Hills Cntry
Hiking Southern New England
Hiking Tennessee
Hiking Texas
Hiking Utah
Hiking Utah's Summits
Hiking Vermont
Hiking Virginia
Hiking Washington
Hiking Wyoming
Hiking Wyoming's Cloud Peak Wilderness
Hiking Wyoming's Wind River Range
Hiking Yellowstone National Park
Hiking Zion & Bryce Canyon
Exploring Canyonlands & Arches
Exploring Hawaii's Parklands

BEST EASY DAY HIKES

Beartooths
Canyonlands & Arches
Cape Cod
Colorado Springs
Glacier & Waterton Lakes
Grand Canyon
Grand Staircase-Escalante/Glen Cny
Grand Teton
Lake Tahoe
Mount Rainier
Mount St. Helens
North Cascades
Olympics
Salt Lake City
Shenandoah
Yellowstone

FALCON®

MORE THAN 5 MILLION COPIES SOLD!

FALCONGUIDES ® Leading the Way ™

PADDLING GUIDES
Floater's Guide to Colorado
Paddling Montana
Paddling Okefenokee
Paddling Oregon
Paddling Yellowstone/Grand Teton

ROCK CLIMBING GUIDES
Rock Climbing Colorado
Rock Climbing Montana
Rock Climbing New Mexico & Texas
Rock Climbing Utah
Rock Climbing Washington

ROCKHOUNDING GUIDES
Rockhounding Arizona
Rockhounding California
Rockhounding Colorado
Rockhounding Montana
Rockhounding Nevada
Rockhound's Guide to New Mexico
Rockhounding Texas
Rockhounding Utah
Rockhounding Wyoming

BIRDING GUIDES
Birding Minnesota
Birding Montana
Birding Northern California
Birding Texas
Birding Utah

FIELD GUIDES
Bitterroot: Montana State Flower
Canyon Country Wildflowers
Central Rocky Mountains Wildflowers
Great Lakes Berry Book
New England Berry Book
Pacific Northwest Berry Book
Plants of Arizona
Rare Plants of Colorado
Rocky Mountain Berry Book
Scats & Tracks of the Pacific Coast States
Scats & Tracks of the Rocky Mountains
Tallgrass Prairie Wildflowers
Western Trees
Wildflowers of Southwestern Utah
Willow Bark and Rosehips

WALKING
Walking Colorado Springs
Walking Denver
Walking Portland
Walking St. Louis
Walking Virginia Beach

FISHING GUIDES
Fishing Alaska
Fishing the Beartooths
Fishing Florida
Fishing Glacier National Park
Fishing Maine
Fishing Montana
Fishing Wyoming
Fishing Yellowstone

To order check with you local bookseller or
call FALCON® at **1-800-582-2665**.
www.FalconOutdoors.com

FALCON®